RESEARCH METHODS
FOR PRODUCT DESIGN

ALEX MILTON
& PAUL RODGERS

Laurence King Publishing

Research Methods for Product Designers

Published in 2013 by
Laurence King Publishing Ltd
361–373 City Road
London EC1V 1LR
Tel: +44 20 7841 6900
Fax: +44 20 7841 6910
email: enquiries@laurenceking.com
www.laurenceking.com

Design © 2013 Laurence King Publishing Limited
Text © 2013 Alex Milton and Paul Rodgers

A catalogue record for this book is available from the British
Library.

ISBN: 978 1 78067 302 8

Series and book design: Unlimited
Project editor: Gaynor Sermon

Printed in China

**Related study material is available on the Laurence King
website at www.laurenceking.com**

LAURENCE KING

CONTENTS

5 MAKING

6 TESTING

INTRODUCTION

AVERAGE HANDSIZE IN FINGER LENGHT

P.S 3 CONTROL

TOP.

SIDE

Introduction

Product designers need a comprehensive understanding of research methods as their day-to-day work routinely involves them observing people, asking questions, searching for information, making and testing ideas, and ultimately generating solutions to problems. The act of research is manifest in the design process. Product design companies now acknowledge the importance of research in their work – indeed, the research methods and particular approaches to design that a company chooses will often differentiate them from others and provide distinctive advantages for their organization, their stakeholders and their clients.

Product design is now a global phenomenon; competition for work today transcends physical, national and cultural borders, and an increasingly challenging economic environment means that product designers have to offer far more in terms of research expertise than they did perhaps 10 or 15 years ago. Huge technological advances in information, computing and manufacturing processes also offer enormous opportunities to product designers, such as the development of 'intelligent' products and services, although these also raise important research questions that need to be dealt with. Product designers are, in many ways, best placed to address these challenges because of the manner in which they apply their design thinking to problems.

This book aims to help you conduct effective and useful research in order to produce better products that users will find pleasure in using. It demonstrates, in a clear, highly visual and structured fashion, how research methods can support product designers and help them address the very real issues the world faces in the twenty-first century. Research methods are a somewhat neglected subject in many product-design courses around the world. The key goal of this book, therefore, is to introduce students to the variety of research methods and tools that can be used, as well as ideas about how and when to deploy them effectively. It contains a number of new and existing methods that will enable you to investigate people, form, lifestyles, services, tools and processes in ways that will make your work more useful and more delightful to their intended audience.

Each method is illustrated in the book with real-world examples in the form of case studies, tutorials and professional advice, all backed by rich visual imagery. The book covers qualitative and quantitative research methods, ethnography, mapping, trend forecasting, cultural diversity, video diaries, cultural probes and many other methods from the wide spectrum of contemporary product design. Interspersed throughout the book are several double-page 'how to' features. These cover the key activities that form the chapter headings of the book, namely Looking, Learning, Asking, Making (Prototyping), Testing, Evaluating and Selecting, and Communicating. The chapter headings themselves in turn provide a clear, structured and informative resource for any product designer involved in research, be that within an educational or industrial context.

Why read this book?

This book is aimed at undergraduate design students and those looking for an introduction to the techniques and methods of product design research. It will provide you with a comprehensive, relevant and visually rich insight into the world of research methods specifically aimed at product designers. The collection of practical case studies and tutorials will inform, help and inspire you to conduct research that will improve the processes, products, services and systems that you will design in the future.

WHAT IS PRODUCT DESIGN RESEARCH?

What is research?

Research can be defined as the search for knowledge, or any systematic investigation into and study of materials and sources in order to establish facts and reach new conclusions. The word 'research' derives from the French *recherché* (to search closely). The primary purpose of applied research (as opposed to basic research) is for discovering, interpreting and developing methods and systems for the advancement of human knowledge on a wide variety of scientific and humanitarian matters relating to our world.

Scientific research provides scientific information and theories to explain the nature and properties of the world around us. It makes practical applications possible. Scientific research can be subdivided into different classifications according to a multitude of academic and application disciplines.

What is design research?

Unlike scientific research, design research is not concerned with what exists but with what ought to be. Research in a design context breaks with the determinisms of the past; it continually challenges, provokes and disrupts the status quo. Whereas scientific research relies on and utilizes abstract mathematical explanations, design research uses representative images, physical models and 3D prototypes in the design and development of things that do not yet exist.

Design research also differs from scientific research, for the most part, in that it is concerned with the plausibility and appropriateness of proposals, while scientific research is concerned with universal truths. Design research tends to produce knowledge that can be defined as trans-disciplinary and heterogeneous in nature and that which seeks to improve the world.

Fig. 1
IDEO Method Cards, developed as a tool to assist in the design process.

Design research investigates the process of designing in all its many fields. It is thus related to design methods in general or for particular disciplines. A primary interpretation of design research is that it is concerned with undertaking research into the design process. Secondary interpretations refer to undertaking research within the process of design. The overall intention is to better understand and improve the processes, products, services and systems being designed. In recent years, design research has evolved into three distinct forms – research into and about design, research as design and research through design. Despite the inevitable overlap between these three categories, there are key distinctions.

1. Research into and about design (history, theory and context) is the most established and still the most common type of work undertaken in design research circles. There are many precedents for this type of scholarly work that look closely at some specific area of practice. Such research, which is often historical, usually employs a method of critical investigation to evaluate and interpret a specific body of art and its signification. In this type of design research, the researcher is unlikely to also be the creator of the work in question. The theoretical perspective taken is generally from a position external to the work being investigated. By reflecting on existing work from outside the creative process, the researcher is able to take a more objective view.

2. Research as design (innovative design methods) is a slightly more contested category. In recent years, a number of design researchers have claimed that making designed objects is, in itself, a process of research. This category refers to the notion that the outcomes of the research are, in some way, embodied entirely in the designed artefacts. The research is likely to involve the gathering and testing of ideas, materials and techniques required to make the artefacts. While research of this type is vital to the production of some original design work, it does not necessarily imply that the artefact makes an 'original contribution to knowledge' in the traditional sense of research. In this category the designer, who is the researcher, is operating almost entirely within the field of interest. The artefacts are unlikely to be interpreted from an external, objective position.

3. Research through design (experimental practice) is considered the taking of 'something' from outside the design work and translating it through the medium. Such work, commonly termed 'practice-based research', is often interdisciplinary in nature and can range from an idea or concept to a new material or process. In this case the researcher will be engaged in making work within a field of interest as well as reflecting on it and contextualizing it. This reflective method engenders a viewpoint that is both internal and external to the subject of the research. In practice-based research new knowledge is generated by a combination of artefacts and the reflection that they engender. In this type of research the uniqueness and/or value will be contained in the nexus between the written text and the designed objects.

Primary and secondary research

Research can be divided into two forms: primary and secondary research. Secondary research involves the summary, collation and/or synthesis of existing research. Primary research involves the design researcher undertaking original research to collect new data through a range of methods and experiments. This enables the researcher to determine the size, nature, timeframe and ultimate goal of the research to be conducted. The drawback of conducting primary research is that the researcher has to create a detailed plan, and the time and cost taken to undertake primary research exceeds that of merely acquiring secondary research data and findings.

Fig. 2
Digital technologies now provide designers with a vast array of computer-based tools to utilize in their research activities.

The iterative design research process

This book presents over 50 design research methods, which have been categorized into seven essential phases, represented by the main chapters: Looking, Learning, Asking, Making (Prototyping), Testing, Evaluating and Selecting, and Communicating. These phases feed into each other through an iterative design process.

Opportunity identification
The earliest stage of the design process, often referred to as 'phase zero', begins with the identification of problems that need to be solved, needs that must be addressed and desires that need to be sated.

Brief and specification
This stage focuses on the construction and analysis of a design brief, identifying the customers' needs, and establishing a comprehensive product design specification (PDS).

Concept design
This stage of the design process involves the creation of a number of different viable concept designs.

Design development
This stage seeks to refine the chosen concept into a product that satisfies the requirements outlined in the PDS.

Detail design
This stage covers the key steps of transforming the chosen concept design into a fully detailed design, with all the dimensions and specifications necessary to make the product specified on a detailed drawing.

Production
The final stage involves how the product is manufactured, and focuses on determining what processes and techniques should be employed. It is important to remember, however, that some stages may occur in a different sequence or may even be omitted altogether, as each product has its own unique set of requirements and the role and scope of design research may, as a result, vary.

As a design passes through the design process, it undertakes an iterative set of cycles, with each cycle consisting of five steps: understand, observe, visualize, review and implement. A cycle begins with the need to truly understand what research activities are required, enabling the design team to understand what needs and/or desires are being met or not. This is followed by a series of observations of end-users, to determine what is actually required. The visualization phase focuses on the production of a series of realized research outputs that enable potential or actual customers to engage with the concepts being developed and then critically analyze and review them with the design team. If the results of this feedback are satisfactory, then the design team can progress to the next stage of the design process. If not, then the design team can undertake the cycle again, prior to progressing.

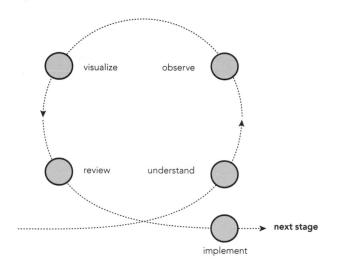

Fig. 3
Each iterative cycle includes four distinct stages, which are usually passed through before either repeating the cycle to gather additional research data, or satisfied with the research undertaken moving on to the next stage of the design process and the next cycle of design research and development.

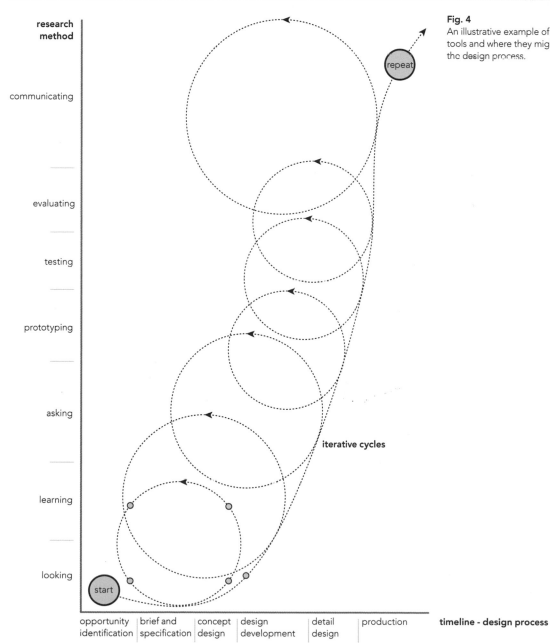

Fig. 4
An illustrative example of research methods and tools and where they might be employed during the design process.

Summary of research methods involved in the design process

This chart details the different stages of the design process and provides a list of the research tools and techniques that may be used, and where to find them in this book. The design process is more cyclical than linear (as shown on page 15) and you may be required to adopt techniques from both earlier and later chapters at every stage.

Research
background stage
exploratory stage

— ethnography

— photo and video diaries

— shadowing

— a day in the life...

— personal belongings

— future forecasting

— product autopsy

— sketching

— cultural probes

— competitor product analysis

— literature review

— web searches

— cultural comparisons

— role playing

— try it yourself

— mind mapping

— sampling

— questionnaires and surveys

— focus groups

— interviews

— marketing and retail research

— intuition

— crowdsourcing

— preparing a presentation

— report creation

The Brief

— cultural probes

— competitor product analysis

— literature review

— web searches

— cultural comparisons

— role playing

— try it yourself

— mind mapping

— sampling

— ethnography

— photo and video diaries

— shadowing

— a day in the life...

— personal belongings

— future forecasting

— product autopsy

— sketching

— questionnaires and surveys

— focus groups

— interviews

— marketing and retail research

— preparing a presentation

— report creation

Concept Design

— questionnaires and surveys

— focus groups

— user narrator

— interviews

— brand DNA analysis

— marketing and retail research

— be your customer

— image and mood boards

— perceptual mapping

— personas

— product collage

— extreme users

— sketching

— photo and video diaries

— cultural probes

— mind mapping

— intuition

— matrix evaluation

— preparing a presentation

— report creation

Design Development

— sketch modelling

— mock ups

— appearance models

— paper prototyping

— quick-and-dirty prototypes

— experience prototyping

— empathy tools

— bodystorming

— rapid prototyping

— photo and video diaries

— a day in the life...

— future forecasting

— product autopsy

— focus groups

— user narration

— interviews

— be your customer

— intuition

— matrix evaluation

Detail Design

— scenario testing

— user trials

— product usability

— material testing

— safety testing

— mock ups

— quick-and-dirty prototypes

— experience prototyping

— rapid prototyping

Production

— checklists

— external decision making

— intuition

— product champion

— crowdsourcing

— matrix evaluation

— preparing a presentation

— report creation

— presentation visuals and models

— engaging the public

Key

Chapter 2 Looking

Chapter 3 Learning

Chapter 4 Asking

Chapter 5 Making

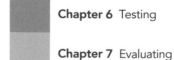

Chapter 6 Testing

Chapter 7 Evaluating

Chapter 8 Communicating

Product design process and methods

Typically, the creation of a new product begins with an idea and ends with the production of a physical artefact. Design research methods support the design and development of new products by helping provide invaluable data, expertise and knowledge through observing, recording and analyzing how consumers interact with the designed world. Research has typically been focused towards the front end of the process, exploring the real needs and desires of end-users. Increasingly designers are realizing the benefit of extensive research throughout the entire product design process, and indeed assessing a product's entire life cycle, from investigating and evaluating the environmental, social and cultural impact of a given product from its inception and manufacture through its lifetime to its final disposal and recycling.

If you intend to minimize or avoid altogether any environmental impact, then you need to consider the impact of a product throughout its entire life cycle – how it is produced, manufactured, transported, packaged, used and disposed of. When designing new products it is useful to storyboard the life story of the product to help identify the possible impacts and events that may occur. This can be useful because the reality of many products' lives does not follow the exact route planned during the design research process, and so alternative eventualities should be considered. You need to establish exactly what the environmental impacts of the product are, or will be, and what they are caused by. By doing this you can identify where the greatest need for improvement lies and so focus your design and research efforts effectively.

Ignoring environmental factors in the design process means that designers are creating financial time bombs for their clients (Edwin Datschefski, 2004). In addition to adopting a sustainable model of design, design researchers also need to ensure they adopt an ethical approach to their research activities. You should ensure that you fully consider the ethical implications of your work and how you conduct your research. You need to ask yourself: Who will own the data? Who can have access to it? Are you inadvertently exploiting the people you want to engage in the research? Creating products is a complicated process, and designers need to be aware of the larger contexts surrounding their work.

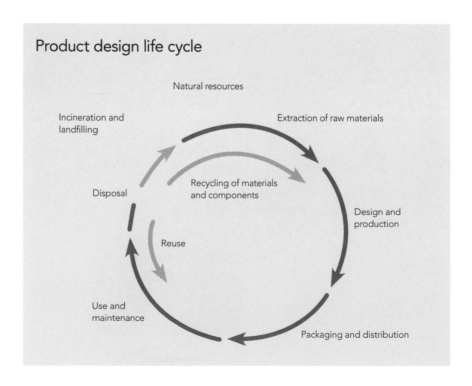

Product design life cycle

Natural resources

Incineration and landfilling

Extraction of raw materials

Recycling of materials and components

Disposal

Design and production

Reuse

Use and maintenance

Packaging and distribution

Analyzing research

The vast majority of research undertaken by designers is qualitative rather than quantitative. This requires the designer to develop a method of categorizing and analyzing the data to uncover and understand the big picture, and highlight the important messages and findings to colleagues, clients and customers.

Once you have conducted a range of research activities and experiments, you need to step back from the methods and processes, and look for the themes, patterns and relationships that are emerging from your research. Look for similarities and differences, and see what different users are saying to you. You may find exceptions, contradictions and surprises, and through questioning, reviewing and analyzing these you should be able to determine the key research findings that will inform your design process.

Whatever type of design research approach you plan, in common with other forms of research, the methods that you employ and the subsequent analysis of the research must be:

— Systematic
— Rigorous
— Critical
— Reflective
— Ethical
— Sustainable
— Communicable to others

Ethics

Ethics in design research is particularly important in an age of digital recording, where it has become relatively easy to collect data such as videos and photographs and post them on the internet. At the start of any research project, you must clarify your research intentions with your participants. That is, what you are looking to find out and why. You need to describe clearly how you are going to use the information you collect and its value to you as a product designer. You must gain permission from your participants if you intend to photograph or video them, and inform them that they can decline to answer specific questions or stop the research at any time. Ensure that the data you collect remains confidential unless you have prior agreement with your participants. Last, but by no means least, make sure you treat people with courtesy at all times, and retain a consistent non-judgemental, relaxed and harmonious relationship with your participants throughout the process.

LOOKING

In order to discover what people really need, want and do rather than just what they say they need, want and do, designers have developed a series of observational research methods. From the stories revealed through examining peoples' emotional attachments to their personal artefacts, to the manufacturing and aesthetic design decisions that are revealed through the forensic analysis of designed products, this chapter examines a number of the research methods used by leading design consultancies. You will discover, through carefully implementing these methods, how looking with a critical eye can help you design and develop great products to address the multitude of complex problems found in modern society.

Ethnography

Ethnography is a research method based on observing people in their natural environment – be that a hospital, a fish factory or a college library – rather than in a formal research setting. Ethnography is a very effective method for making sense of the complexities of people and cultures. It allows you to immerse yourself in other people's lives and witness patterns of behaviour within real-world contexts. Studying what people do rather than what they say they do provides a richer, more realistic overview of how people live, work and play. The aim of an ethnographic study is to learn from (rather than study) people in a particular cultural group – the intention being to understand those peoples' worldview. If conducted well, ethnography can provide you with a detailed, in-depth insight into people's behaviours, beliefs and preferences, and how they operate in their day-to-day lives.

In a design context ethnography helps designers create more compelling products, services, spaces and systems because they have been based on real observations of people.

Fig. 1
A sequence of photos highlighting the work of an automobile technician. Observing and recording visually what people do provides a rich and realistic snapshot of how people work.

The following points should help ensure you conduct a good ethnography:

1. Remember ethnography is not only about asking questions, but listening to the answers.
2. Ethnography should delve deeply into the lives of a few people rather than study many people superficially.
3. Ethnography involves studying people's behaviours and experiences holistically in daily life.
4. Think carefully about what questions you will ask and how you will go about translating large amounts of data into concise and compelling findings.
5. Make good use of video, photos and other visual materials.
6. Avoid merely listing facts and focus instead on telling stories from the data you have collected.
7. Reflect carefully on the data you have collected and make connections.

Ethnography is a very powerful method and one a designer shouldn't dismiss lightly. If you want to design a product that will be accepted, used and loved by people, then you need to understand their day-to-day lives, rituals and habits first. Ethnography is a fluid process incorporating the collection, interpretation and presentation of data, which originates from the disciplines of social and cultural anthropology. Typically, in-depth, semi-structured interviews are employed in which respondents are encouraged to use their own vocabulary and participate as in a discussion. These interviews help uncover people's language, behaviour, thoughts and interactions with their products, environments and services. Several variances of ethnography are commonly used in product design today. These include digital ethnography, where digital tools (e.g. cameras, laptops, the internet) can be used to speed up the process of data collection, analysis and presentation, and rapid ethnography, a method of estimation that fits well with the product design and development process, where designers tend to need answers in hours or days, not weeks, months or years.

Fig. 2
A visual array of research methods that can be used in product design (courtesy of IDEO Methods Cards)

Madalena 6 z z z

18
Med student
1st year

15m

No sports
Social life: at the library
Lives with her parents

The canteen queue is huge. Madalena will have to speed up her lunch.

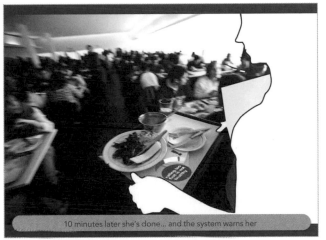

10 minutes later she's done... and the system warns her

...and she heads to the library again

BIBLIOTECA

Study hours
yesterday
1h27

Last week

Malena is ready for another 4 hour session...

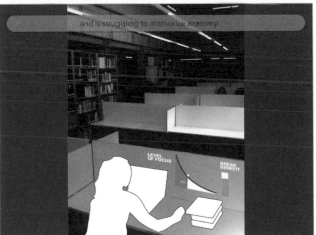

and is struggling to memorize anatomy.

LEVEL
OF FOCUS

BREAK
BENEFIT

Fig. 3
Video diary recording the activity of a first year
medical student. This research was undertaken to
determine the pace of life of students with a view
to developing a 'widget' that gives feedback on
their habits and guidance on how to have a more
balanced lifestyle.

Photo and video diaries

Photo and video diaries are a highly effective way of collecting observational, visually rich data. They allow design researchers to gain detailed insights into an individual's experience with a particular product or activity. A key advantage of photo and video diaries is that they help capture spontaneous and significant events and experiences in a person's natural surroundings, minimizing the amount of retrospective time between an actual experience and the person's account of the experience in their diary. Photo and video diaries provide an excellent way of studying and capturing significant moments in the day-to-day lives of people in natural settings, such as family birthday parties, breakfast, watching TV, reading the newspaper, cleaning dishes and bedtime rituals.

Research participants are asked to undertake a series of tasks on their own in their home or place of work and requested to photograph or film this as they do so. Each participant is typically given a set of instructions or prompts to follow. For example, participants might be asked to prepare a typical evening meal every day for one week and record their activity in a series of photographs, supported by written comments.

The participant would usually be asked to avoid taking photos of family members and friends during the study for confidentiality reasons. During a typical week-long study, the participant might be asked to carefully record the number, date and time of each photo, and where it was taken, together with any other comments they wish to make, such as why they chose that particular cooking utensil, why they chose to cook the food in that particular way, and so on. The participant would be asked to try to fill in the diary at least once a day for the full seven days.

Photo and video diaries give us access to a person's world beyond what we might be able to get in a face-to-face meeting, enabling us to see what they do in multiple locations, at different times and in a variety of situations.

Figs. 4 & 5
Photo and video diaries enable researchers to collect valuable visual data, providing insights into an individual's experience with a particular product or activity over a set period of time.

Shadowing

Shadowing is a method that involves a researcher closely following an individual or small team within an organization over a predefined period of time. The researcher 'shadows' the target individual from the moment they begin their working day until the time when they leave for home. This can include hours of stationary observation while the person being shadowed writes at his or her desk, runs between buildings for a series of meetings or attends dinners held for clients. Shadowing is typically conducted over a number of consecutive or non-consecutive days for up to a month. Studies can be focused on a single role in several companies or on a number of roles within the same company.

Throughout the shadowing period the researcher asks questions that will prompt a running commentary from the person being shadowed. Some of the questions will be for clarification, such as what was said on the other end of a phone call, or the meaning of a departmental joke. Other questions will be intended to reveal purpose, such as why a particular line of argument was pursued in a meeting, or what the current operational priorities are. During shadowing the researcher will write an almost continuous set of field notes. They will record the times and content of conversations, the answers to the questions they asked and as much of the running commentary as possible. They will note the body language and moods of the person they are shadowing.

At the end of the shadowing period the researcher will have a rich, dense and comprehensive set of data, which gives a detailed, first-hand and multifaceted picture of the role, approach, philosophy and tasks of the subject. This research data can then be analyzed in the same way as any other qualitative data, to provide invaluable insights, which can inform the creation of a detailed design brief.

When conducting a shadowing study you should always consider the following:

1. Never go in cold. It is important to spend time getting to know both the organization and, to a lesser extent, the individuals you will be shadowing. If you don't know the names of your subject's boss, work colleagues and husband, not to mention the major product lines and suppliers, your notes will not be very meaningful at the start of your shadowing.

2. Use a small, hardback notebook and a pen to keep a research account (and make sure you have a supply of spares). This will allow you to make notes wherever you are. Tape recorders are sometimes not practical for shadowing due to background noise.

3. Write down as much as you can. This is especially important at the start of a project when you can still see the organization as an outsider. Settings, the meaning of acronyms, how meetings make you feel, relationships and your first impressions of people (and how these change) are all relevant data.

4. Get into the habit of making a daily tape transcript of your research notes. This makes it easier to decipher what you have been writing at speed and helps keep your accounts rich and detailed. It also helps to preserve your own thoughts and impressions, which will change very quickly once you start to lose your beginner perspective.

5. Plan your data management. Decide how you are going to record, manage and analyze your data before going into the field.

A day in the life

'A day in the life' is a useful research method for revealing unanticipated issues inherent in the routines and circumstances people may experience on a daily basis. It is an intensive research method that aims to provide a representative snapshot, in contrast to other observational research methods such as shadowing, which aim to build up a picture over a longer sustained period of study.

Designers using this method follow a 'performer' (someone who regularly performs the task) for a period of time, cataloguing the performer's activities and experiences throughout a typical day. The technique gets its name because the research is conducted over the course of a day. Typically, this will be for a full 24 hours or possibly a more conventional eight-hour, 9-to-5 work day. Using this technique, you act like a fly on the wall, observing and recording everything that the performer does, as well as the environment in which the performer interacts.

Fig. 6
Following an individual from the moment they begin their working day until the time when they leave can give a rich and comprehensive view of the role, approach, philosophy and tasks of the subject being shadowed.

For example, this might involve following and observing the work of an automobile technician in their garage or recording the daily activities undertaken by a dentist in their surgery. You might decide to record the activities in a handwritten journal and/or film the performer. In some instances, you may elect to follow an 'expert' and a 'novice' performer. By comparing their lives, you can understand how different levels of skill, aptitude and experience can affect how people navigate their world and their use of a range of products. You can then apply this knowledge to creating 'design interventions' that might help disadvantaged people.

In addition to observing the performer's behaviour and environment, you should also interview them throughout the day – at times that will not intrude on the work being observed. Interviews can provide insights into decisions that a performer makes and other behaviours that might not be visible or might not be clear from observing, as well as revealing the challenges that the performer faces on a day-to-day basis and the motivations underlying their work. When conducting 'A day in the life' research you should note down your personal impressions and any queries you may have that can be answered through subsequent primary research activities.

Fig. 7
'A day in the life' study, shadowing a nurse over the course of a full working day. The researcher acts like a fly on the wall, observing and recording everything that the subject does, as well as the environment in which she interacts.

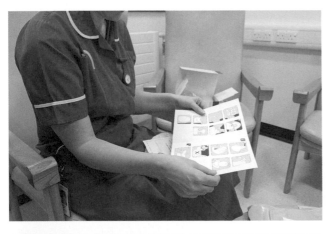
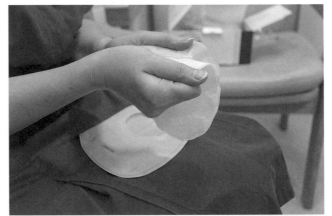
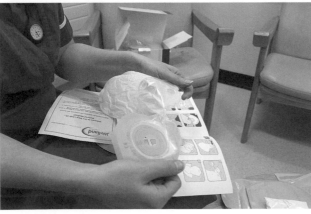
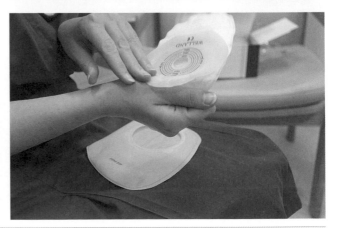

Personal belongings

This research method involves asking people what personal belongings are important to them in order to ascertain the things that are valued by people and identify any patterns of use among them. Owners and users often invest products with a meaning that transcends their functionality, developing a patina of memories that can transform a seemingly mundane object into a treasured possession. This research method reveals how users assign personal meaning, symbolism and value to products. Information gathered through this method can then be used to inform the creation of products that address consumers' wants, rather than mere needs. In today's consumerist society, if the designs that we purchase, use and covet reflect who we are, then designers need to examine our relationships with our belongings. Through observation, designers can discover how people become emotionally attached to products, and apply these observations to create products that will be cherished. Valued personal belongings can be broadly categorized as follows, although they are not mutually exclusive.

Collectively cherished products

Iconic products and brands attract dedicated collectors who often form owners' clubs and fan sites to share mutual admiration and interest. These organizations and societies are fantastic repositories of research material for designers, and have been widely consulted when companies have chosen to develop 'retro' products that mine our collective memories, such as the new Fiat 500 or Star Wars film merchandise.

Fig. 8
The 'personal belongings' method involves asking people what belongings are important to them. This can reveal the things that are highly valued by people and identify how they assign personal meanings, symbolism and value to their products.

Individually cherished products

Everyday products can often gain emotional value through personal association and use. Heirlooms are products passed down from one generation to the next, and represent memories that transcend function or monetary value. Memorabilia and souvenirs always contain a built-in emotional value, such as the memory of a past holiday or significant personal event. Designers actively explore people's relations with their keepsakes, mementos and belongings in order to discover methods of creating products that foster meaningful relationships with their owners. Designers are often avid collectors themselves, and source obscure material to help inspire their design practice. From the collection of vintage toys and mechanisms sourced in flea markets and through eBay, to priceless collections of design art and mid-century modern furniture, designers' personal belongings can offer an invaluable research resource.

Future forecasting

Product designers need to continually strive to understand what their current and target customers want, how they currently use a product and to forecast what they will desire next season and beyond. Forecasting future trends is a key part of marketing and design strategies in the product design industry. Anticipating where the market will be in the future gives the designer an important research tool. While timely and regular market and research data can help to identify consumer needs, there is also a real need to anticipate future consumer wants, needs and desires.

Future forecasting can identify future aesthetic preferences, such as seasonal colours, materials and textures, through to developing speculative scenarios and products that aim to address long-term issues such as global warming. The gestation time to bring a product to market is such that the global conditions impacting on its success can alter from conception to product launch. With stockmarket crashes, socio-cultural trends and fashion moving so fast, expert research into future trends is becoming ever more important to the design industry and process.

Trend forecasters and futurologists (specialists who postulate possible futures by evaluating past and present trends) are commonly working to timescales of 18 months in advance in rapid-turnover fields such as fashion and textiles, to ten years or more in areas such as car design. Designers are required to

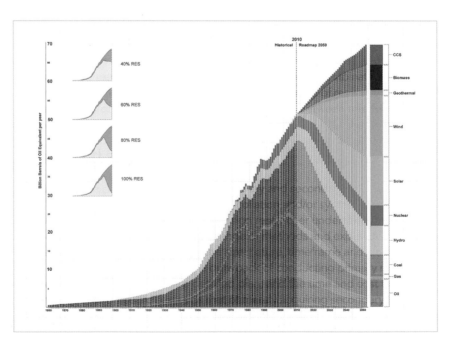

Fig. 9
The future forecasting method helps designers identify future aesthetic preferences, such as seasonal colours, materials and textures, through to developing speculative scenarios and products that aim to address long-term issues such as global warming.

analyze a wide range of subjective visual data and statistical information gathered from interviews with key stakeholders, reports from photographic trend spotters, trade shows, exhibitions, selected key media and relevant social media. By distilling this information, they are able to identify emerging trends and extrapolate likely scenarios. These forecasts are then presented in the form of scenarios, stories and visual mood and image boards.

Trend spotting

A trend by definition is something that has already begun, and trends are therefore spotted rather than created. Once spotted, a trend can then be analyzed in detail, to identify its qualities and probable development. Trends are commonly presented through the following perspectives:

— **Commercial trends**: You can identify future economic trends and potential market developments and opportunities by critically reviewing sales figures, trade shows and market reports.
— **Design trends**: By collating a library of materials and samples you can predict design trends for identifiable periods. You can also use 'associational' words to summarize potential trends.
— **Visual trends**: You can create an informed overview of current trends and developments by creating a visual survey culled from the design press, product launches, trade fairs, books, magazines and the output of numerous cutting-edge design groups.

Trend spotting can help designers identify future economic trends and potential market opportunities. This is typically undertaken by reviewing phenomena such as trade shows, the design press, magazines, market reports, and the output of numerous cutting-edge design groups.

Fig. 10
Fiona Jenvey is Chief Executive and founder of Mudpie fashion forecasting agency, whose services include the publication of seasonal trend prediction packages, trend presentations at global trade events, and working with manufacturers around the world, offering a consultancy service.

Scenarios

Design scenarios allow designers not just to predict the future, but also to raise questions and issues about it. Many product design companies now present scenarios through the medium of film, which can help garner subjective qualitative consumer responses from a range of audiences. Companies such as Philips use design scenarios not just to predict the future, but also to raise questions and issues about it, and to propose ideas and solutions that will enhance people's lives. The use of short films helps to avoid the trap of having future forecasts dismissed as science fiction, by revealing speculative products, but demonstrating them being used by ordinary people in realistic future contexts.

By creating speculative design concepts that are communicated through narratives, exhibitions, images and films, companies can propose design directions and garner subjective qualitative consumer responses from a range of audiences. Future forecasting and trend spotting enable designers to predict and interpret the vital implications of user behaviour and develop future scenarios informed by hard data and expert observation to give their clients the confidence that they are making the right decision.

Figs. 11 & 12
Using scenarios to research and develop a range of digital musical instruments. Early research in this project studied how people reacted to various forms, and user scenarios were storyboarded to better understand the potential product use.

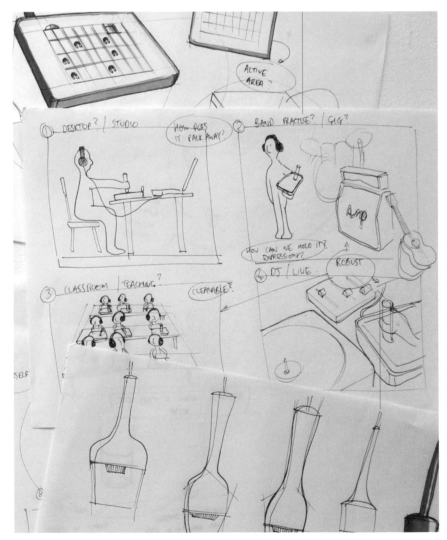

Product autopsy

Product autopsy is a method used to gain a better understanding of the design decisions that have been made in an existing product, such as the materials used, the manufacturing techniques and processes used in the product's development, why certain components have been used, and why aesthetic decisions on the product's form, colour and finish have been taken. A product autopsy is also a valuable method for reviewing how well a product has functioned during its life and how well it has aged.

In conducting a product autopsy you try to find out more about the product's life – how long it has lived, how well it has worked, which component parts have been damaged or worn and which have lasted. A product autopsy begins with a rigorous visual analysis of the artefact, paying particular attention to any visible signs of wear and tear or damage. Next, the product is carefully disassembled. This will usually begin with the removal of a tough exterior casing to reveal many more fragile components and materials inside. It is typical, for example, for a mobile phone to consist of over 30 major components, including parts such as a liquid crystal display (LCD), electronics boards, electro-luminescent (EI) film, a microphone, a speaker assembly, a display screen, battery and keypad.

Once inside, the product autopsy should be carried out gently and thoroughly in an attempt to find out where the constituent parts have come from, how they might be reused or disposed of after the autopsy is over, how each constituent part was made, who made it, what its specific purpose is and how well it has fulfilled its role in the overall function of the product. The point of conducting a product autopsy is to learn how products have been developed initially, then how they have matured, degraded and expired so as to make better decisions regarding material selections, spray coatings, electronics packaging, manufacturing processes and design choices for future products. As a designer you must remember that it is not merely a great aesthetic that makes a good product, but longevity and user experience, which gain trust and ultimately build a loyal following. So your job as a designer is not only to design beautiful products, but also to ensure you design for the elegant degradation of your products.

Fig. 13
Carefully taking a product apart to conduct a 'product autopsy' allows researchers to better understand why certain design decisions were made, and allows them to see how a product's components have fared in terms of wear-and-tear.

Sketching

Sketching is a key research and development tool that enables designers to evaluate their ideas on paper, storing concepts for later discussion, manipulation and iterative development. The act of sketching works as a means of firming up a research idea; it allows designers to wrestle with design possibilities, and attempt to give form and meaning to an idea.

Usually designers will start generating their ideas with a pen or pencil and paper. Most designers utilize these tools at the early stages of the design process because of the immediacy of the sketching process, the freedom provided and the temporary nature (sketches can easily be erased, revised and redrawn) of pencils and paper. A designer also annotates his or her sketches – notes will act as aides-memoire for the designer and also help identify key points so that his or her ideas can be communicated to members of the design team and all the stakeholders involved. Concept sketches allow us to see the designer's mind at work and fall into two broad categories, as follows.

Thematic sketches
These types of sketch are the initial exploratory visions of how a proposed design may look. They tend to be drawn in a wilfully fluid, dynamic and expressive manner, free from constraint. Thematic sketches should convey the product's physical form, characteristics and overall aesthetic. Such drawings often rely on a series of visual conventions that, to an uninformed eye or critical client, may need explanation.

Fig. 14
Sketched plan for an exhibition at Italy's Triennale Design Museum.

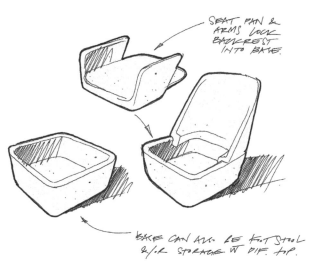

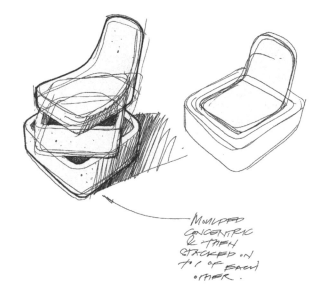

Fig. 15
Sketches for Tom Dixon's EPS Chair.

Fig. 16
Concept sketches of Tokujin Yoshioka's 'Invisibles'
range of furniture. These capture the style and
feel of the designs without too much detail.

Fig. 17
Early sketches for designer Patricia Urquiola's new
Foliage Sofa and Comback Chair for Kartell.

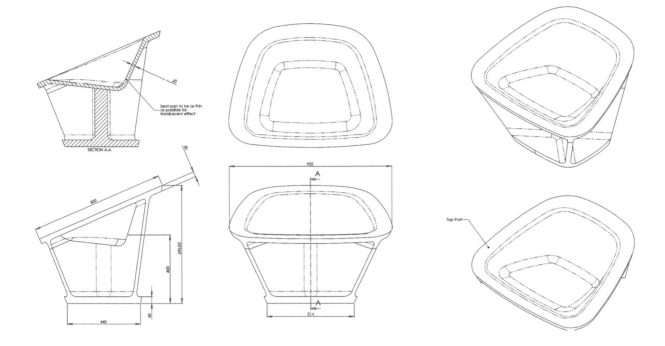

Fig. 18
(Above) Technical drawings of Tom Dixon's EPS Chair. These have been refined from earlier sketches to be used in the manufacturing process.

Fig. 19
(Opposite page) Detailed CAD drawings of Pearson Lloyd's Cobi Chair, with sketches and notes added to develop the backrest rib detail.

Fig. 20
(Below right) Schematic sketches used to develop a computer tablet concept.

Schematic sketches

These sketches place less emphasis on the external styling or appearance of a design, and more on defining and working within a 'package'. This term is used to describe the fixed dimensional parameters of a design, including vital data such as off-the-shelf components to be used and ergonomic considerations.

The real secret to sketching is realizing that you should be as economical as possible with your marks on paper, while still creating an informative visual. Being able to sketch convincingly is vital for the designer, in order to communicate design concepts quickly and present concepts to users, colleagues and clients. Once a concept has been settled upon, the designer is then able to move on to the production of presentation visuals to sell the design to clients or investors, and to involve target users in design critiques of these visuals.

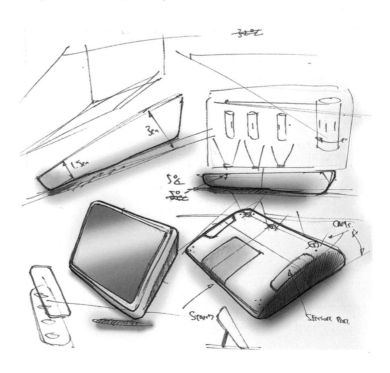

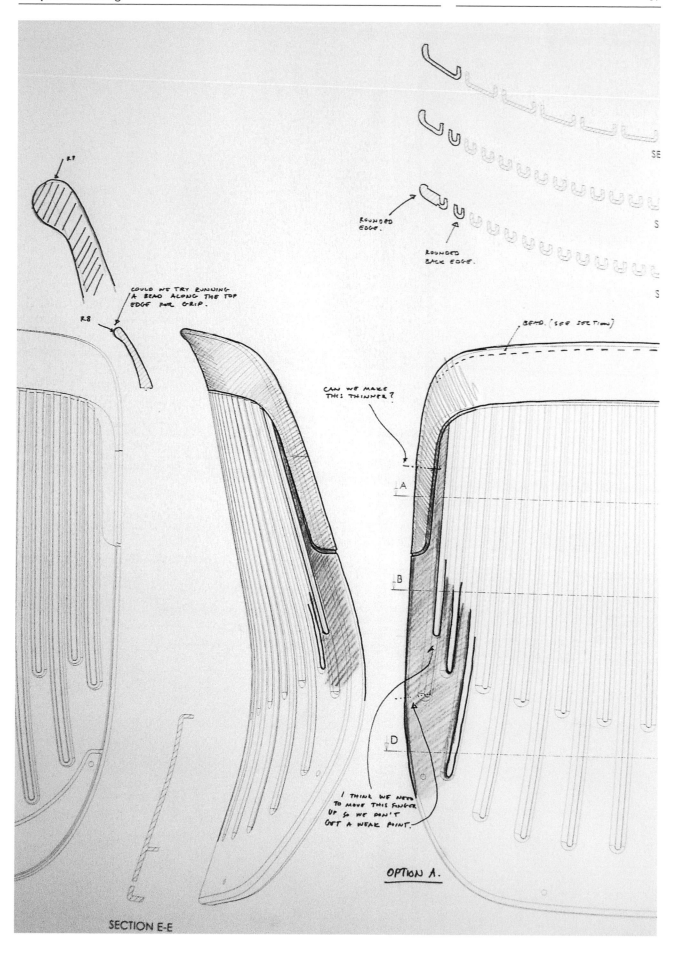

SECTION E-E

Case Study

IDEO Havaianas Tote

Introduction

The Havaianas brand embodies what it means to be Brazilian – that is, free-spirited, with a zest for life and an instinct for improbable combinations.

The company first designed inexpensive cloth shoes for Brazilian coffee farmers in 1907; today it offers nearly 20 product lines worldwide and sells 162 million pairs of flip-flops a year. Scan the pathways and streets the world over and you'll find Havaianas' iconic footwear on everyone from celebrities like Gisele Bundchen and Beyonce Knowles to everyday consumers who appreciate affordable, versatile shoes.

Objective

With 60 years of consistent growth, Havaianas came to IDEO to help extend its brand into a new product category. The company wanted to offer a line of tote bags that shared the simple pleasure and boldness of its flip-flops, starting with ways in which people could carry their Havaianas around.

Methods

To imagine what these Havaiana accessories might look like, IDEO first sought to capture the essence of the brand by understanding its tight connection to Brazil's national identity. The team interviewed citizens from a variety of demographic and socioeconomic backgrounds and found that they all had vibrant spirits and an appreciation for simplicity, authenticity, play, enjoyment and physical comfort. The team also conducted additional research in Australia, India, London and Paris.

The IDEO team also ran a series of 'handstorms', or bag-making brainstorm sessions that led to hundreds of prototypes. Each was considered in relation to the brand vision for Havaianas. Working with a seamstress, the team tried various shapes and materials. In the end they developed a consistent design language that echoed the look and feel of Havaianas flip-flops with textural and visual cues.

Results

The resulting line of modular bags was designed to meet the needs of Havaianas customers and its retailers. The bags' style is relaxed, individualistic, and uncomplicated. The colours, based on a palette curated from photographs taken throughout Brazil, capture the fun and the vibrancy of the country. The commercial rollout of the bags put great emphasis on staying true to Havaianas's Brazilian heritage. By introducing the bag in Brazil, Havaianas allowed its flip-flop fans at home to be the first to enjoy the product. Havaianas unveiled the bags at Sao Paulo's fashion week in June 2008. The totes were rolled out elsewhere in 2009.

Below: The Havaianas Zip P bag in brilliant yellow.

Top left: Myriad photos of Brazil provided inspiration.

Above: Real-world images inspired the colour palette for the new line of bags.

Left: Working with a seamstress, IDEO tried various shapes and materials.

Bottom: Some of the sample materials used for prototyping.

Case Study

Sense Worldwide

Introduction

Regence is a century-old American health insurance company that has grown into a multi-million-dollar 'blue chip' business. The business was due to face fundamental change as a result of the US government's planned healthcare reforms.

Objective

The company knew change was needed, but were unsure of where to start. As health insurance in the US is almost entirely business-to-business and sales driven, becoming a consumer-conscious business was a step into the unknown.

Methods

Sense Worldwide started by asking the company a series of questions in order to get to grips with the industry as Regence saw it. They then asked the company to consider some additional points of view so as to get the core team aligned around a set of areas of investigation that would enable the problem to be explored from the perspective of various stakeholders. Adopting an ethnographic approach, Sense Worldwide interviewed 50 consumers and employers across four US states. As well as talking to key target markets, they talked to extreme users (in this case, people who were refusing health insurance, taking trips to the Far East for operations and

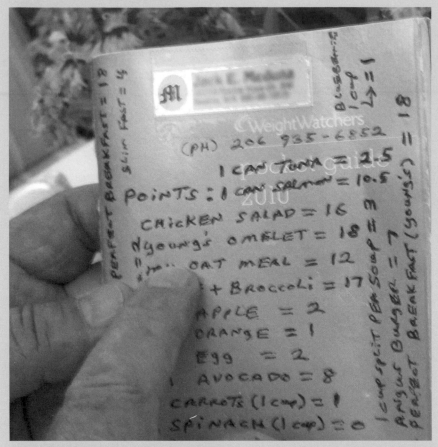

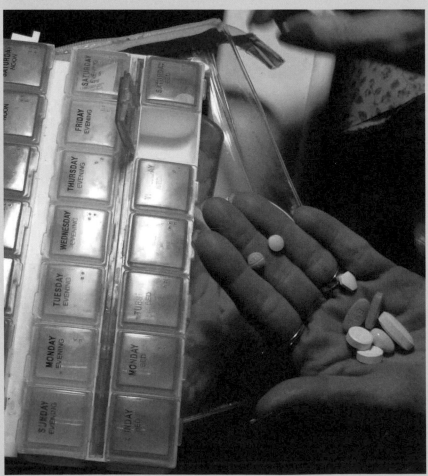

ordering prescription drugs from Mexico). They also talked to super users with chronic conditions, employers from small and medium-sized enterprises (SMEs), large corporations and the government.

Results

Sense Worldwide's brand master plan was the restructuring of the entire organization around a new holding company, with health insurance becoming just one part of its subsidiaries. Alongside a chain of gyms and an online wellbeing programme, among other subsidiaries, Regence now offer to look after people in a more holistic way.

Ethnographic research gave Sense Worldwide an insight into a variety of different consumers' approaches to health, diet and taking medication. This allowed them to help Regence connect with their customers and tailor their health insurance plans to suit their target markets.

How to conduct an ethnographic study

There are several important stages that you will need to consider and complete when undertaking an ethnographic study.

1. The first task involves defining the problem. You need to identify and define the key issues you are facing. You might have a specific question or just a general sense that more information is needed on a particular topic. Usually, however, the research question you ask will be fairly open-ended. Your objective is to observe, describe and interpret the situation you are studying. Your main research question might have several sub-questions that will be more specific in nature. Remember the key aim here is to examine the everyday activities and behaviours of people in their natural surroundings over a prolonged period of time.

2. The next stage requires that you identify and locate the people you wish to study. Who are the people who can most likely provide insights on the questions you are asking? Is it a particular group of people who use certain products or act in a particular fashion? Is it a particular cross-section of people that live and work in a specific environment, culture or geographical location?

3. Next you need to carefully plan your approach. You need to decide how you will actually carry out your observations and interactions with the people you wish to study. You also need to decide how much time will you allocate to each task, person and situation. You should develop a set of questions and prompts that will act as a consistent framework for your study. Make sure

you also build enough time into the ethnographic study to allow your subjects opportunities to show what they do, what they value and how they undertake their day-to-day tasks.

4. The next stage involves the vitally important task of collecting data. This requires you to concentrate carefully on the task at hand, take everything in, use all of your five senses (not just your eyes and ears) and to be generally curious. The attitudes, mannerisms, language and interactions among the group you are studying are all very important. You must take a particular interest in how what you are observing might support or contradict commonly held assumptions. The collection of data at this stage will likely require you to take photographs, make video and audio recordings, and take handwritten notes and sketches.

5. The penultimate stage is the crucial task of reflection and analysis of data and interpreting opportunities. This is a demanding part of any ethnographic study. One of the key objectives in this stage is to go deeper than the more obvious insights derived from the observations and data collected in the previous stage. The analysis of ethnographic data can be a time-consuming activity. You need to be able to reflect carefully upon what you have experienced and observed during the study. This should always be done away from the members of the culture under study. The outcome of this stage might include design principles, films, personas and user scenario stories that can be told to multiple audiences, and might also include possible future steps.

6. The final stage involves the ethnographic research write-up and sharing of insights. Here, the insights that have been generated by the study are used to help inform the design decisions that will need to be made for the product being developed. This information should be presented in a highly visual way that will be much more likely to intrigue, inspire and engage your clients and colleagues, and can be communicated using techniques such as storytelling.

Observing people in their natural environment – in this instance a tree surgeon – provides a very good sense of the complexities of their day-to-day lives within real-world contexts.

How to conduct a day-in-the-life study

A day-in-the-life reveals unanticipated issues inherent in the daily routines and circumstances people encounter. In this example, a number of issues are identified in the way engineers install solar panels in residential properties.

Here are a number of tips to ensure that you get the most out of the 'A day in the life' research method.

1. The first thing to consider before undertaking this type of study is to prepare beforehand. You should never start cold. It is vitally important that you spend some time getting to know both the environment of the organization where you will be carrying out the study and the person that you will be following closely. You need to identify the key individuals that will be integral to the study. For example, who is the line manager of the individual you are shadowing for a day? Who are the individual's key colleagues, and what are their names? What are the major work roles and activities of the person you are shadowing? What environments, interactions and relationships are crucial to this person in their day to-day life?

2. Second, you need to keep meaningful notes. At times during the study your notes will be inarticulate and insignificant. This is fairly common and you may experience this at various points during the day. You should therefore plan how you are going to record, manage and analyze the data you wish to collect before going into the field. You might wish to structure the day around significant activities such as formal meetings, phone calls, presentations and so on. Alternatively, you might decide to break the day down into hourly slots. You might also restrict the time shadowing the individual to less than 24 hours – for example, you may shadow an office worker between the hours of 9am and 5pm.

3. Third, you must prepare the recording equipment that you will rely on to capture your data during the day. This will likely include a notebook and pen for jotting down notes and sketches, a camera for capturing significant moments in the person's day, and video and audio equipment for capturing important sequences and conversations. Any equipment will need to be compact; you must ensure that it doesn't get in the way of the person going about their normal daily activities.

4. Next, you must strive to capture as much data as you can – write down as much as possible, take lots of photos, and record significant moments using video and audio devices throughout the day. This is particularly important at the start of the day, when you can still observe the person, their organization and their work colleagues as a relative 'outsider'. The environments you experience during the day, the meaning of any work-related acronyms or industrial language, how meetings make you feel, the relationships among key workers and your first impressions of people (and how these change throughout the day) are all valuable forms of data and should be logged quickly and carefully.

5. When carrying out this kind of study it can also be helpful to discuss your research with a colleague or a friend. This individual should not be associated with the study in any way and should not be from the organization where the study is being carried out. Having an individual who is entirely neutral can provide vital moral support; they can also bring an entirely fresh perspective to your research.

6. Another good habit to get into is making regular data transcriptions of the research you are collecting. This makes it easier to make sense of what you have been writing at speed at particular points in the day and it also helps keep your accounts rich and detailed. Data dumps also help to preserve your thoughts and impressions at particular moments in time, which are subject to change as you lose your 'beginner' perspective over time.

7. Finally, you need to decide what to do with your data and how to make the best sense of it. A common approach for analyzing qualitative data is content analysis, which usually involves a couple of key steps: (i) categorizing the information, identifying major themes and/or patterns and organizing them into coherent categories and (ii) identifying patterns and connections within and between categories. For example, categories might be theme-based (e.g. sleeping, walking, resting, working) or time-based (e.g. early morning, mid-morning, lunchtime, afternoon, early evening, late evening).

LEARNING

Designers can learn what people really need, want and do by looking closely at and learning from existing products, systems and services. Using careful and comprehensive information-gathering techniques, such as competitor product analysis, literature reviews and internet searches, designers can analyze and learn to identify patterns and insights into the behaviours of people and how they relate to and utilize their products. Furthermore, by employing role playing and research methods such as 'Try it yourself', designers can learn first-hand what using a particular product in a specific context feels like. A designer can learn a lot from the past by careful research, while at the same time keeping an eye on future developments.

Cultural Probes

Cultural probes are designed to provoke, expose and capture the inspirational responses that describe an individual's relationship to designed products, spaces, systems and services. They are used to learn about people's lives as they watch television, search the internet for information, get ready for work in the morning, and communicate with family and friends, and so provide designers with rich data that can be used in the design of future products and services.

A cultural probe kit typically includes items for gathering a variety of information in a creative manner, such as an instant, disposable or digital camera, maps, sheets of paper, stickers, a diary, postcards, a voice recorder, pens and post-it notes. The contents of a kit depend largely on what kind of information you want to collect, and on the materials and equipment the participants are familiar with. People respond positively to good-looking, interesting kits, so careful planning, preparation and usage of good-quality materials is advisable.

Cultural probe kits can contain more than a dozen objects, each specifically selected to support the collection of myriad fragmentary insights into an individual's day-to-day life, wishes, needs and aspirations.

Fig. 1
An example of a cultural probes kit containing cameras, writing materials, envelopes and a diary.

Using cultural probes involves a number of discrete stages, including:
— Planning what material (e.g. text, images) needs to be collected and how.
— Recruiting participants relevant to the design project.
— Selecting volunteers (e.g. teenagers, gardeners, teachers).
— Creating cultural probes (i.e. the objects and materials to be included in the pack), then deploying them – usually leaving the participant to complete the activities in the pack in their own time.
— Retrieving and analyzing the probes.
— Designing the future product, service or system by processing the information collected in support of it.

Cultural probes are generally utilized at the concept-development stage of the design process to help support the definition of user needs and propose design ideas. One potential downside to using them, however, is that the amount of information processing and data analysis required can be time-intensive.

Cultural probes are particularly suited to design projects of an experimental nature – for example, where designers might be dealing with unfamiliar situations and need to understand local cultures and rituals so that their design proposals are not deemed inappropriate, irrelevant or arrogant. In short, cultural probes are intended to lead user groups towards unexpected ideas without pressurizing them into any specific singular design proposal. Questions and prompts within a cultural probe kit typically pose open-ended questions and requests, such as:

— What is your favourite room in your home?
— What you will wear today?
— Use the camera enclosed to take six to ten pictures to tell us your story.
— Use the camera enclosed to take one picture of something boring.
— Tell us a place where you would like to go but can't.
— Tell us about your favourite product.

Researchers will deliberately word any questions obliquely, to provide users with as much room as possible to respond.

Fig. 2
Simon's Swapbox is a digital variation of a cultural probe. The rebuilt mobile phone inside is limited to only four working modes: message display, sound recording, video recording and photo mode. The researcher sends short messages to participants via an Internet server, who answer by taking photos and videos or recording sounds and stories and sending messages are back. Here the box is being used to record daily eating habits.

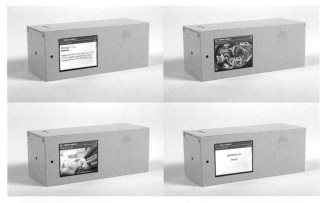

Competitor product analysis

A competitor product analysis is the process by which a product and its competitors in a specific market sector are examined and evaluated with respect to a predefined set of criteria. A competitor and/or analogous products analysis identifies the strengths and weaknesses of competing or similar products and/or services and is usually undertaken before starting to develop any design prototypes. This is a very useful way of evaluating and comparing the product being developed alongside its main competitors. A competitor product analysis helps to establish a range of both qualitative and quantitative criteria, including functional requirements and more subjective performance levels. Catalogues, trade magazines and the likes of the *Which?* magazine and website (formerly known as the Consumers' Association) are all good sources of details for competitor and analogous products.

Depending on the time and resources available, you begin the analysis by selecting an appropriate number of competing products to evaluate and compare. You should also determine exactly who the main competitors and their products are. (It is a good idea to ask a range of people, including users, designers, domain experts and marketing specialists, to review the list of competitor products to ensure that the most important competitors are represented.) Awareness of the product's intended use is vitally important, too, as it will identify the users, the tasks and the context in which the product will be used. A fundamental mistake in competitor product analysis is to focus too much on the technology and not on the user needs to be addressed. So you need to carefully define what products are already on the marketplace that satisfy the user needs you are interested in.

The competing products are then put through a series of typical tasks. By recording how each product performs during each task you will be able to evaluate each in turn by asking, for example: How easy (perhaps on a scale of 1 to 5) is the product to use? How reliable is it? How much does it cost? How long do I need to charge the product's batteries before they are fully charged?

Having established the strengths and weaknesses of each product, you will be able to generate a short summary of all of the competing products and their overall market position. This summary can then be used to develop a list of issues that need to be addressed in order to compete effectively in the marketplace. The summary may also help generate a list of desirable functions and/or features that the product being developed needs to include that were not considered at the outset of the project.

Fig. 3
A range of competitor products in the smart phone market.

Fig. 4
A design researcher reviewing relevant literature.
Books, reports, conference papers, journal and
trade magazine articles, and many other forms of
output can provide an informed and critical
account related to a particular design issue or area
of exploration.

Literature reviews

A literature review examines published scholarly articles, papers, books, scientific
reports and other relevant sources (academic dissertations, conference papers,
trade magazine articles and so on) that provide an informed description, summary
or critical account related to a particular design issue or area of exploration. The
purpose of a literature review is to gain an overview of the significant literature
published on a particular topic that will allow the design team to develop an
informed opinion and perspective on the subject. It may, therefore, range widely in
size and scope, depending on the nature of the design project being undertaken.
A typical review may take in patent searches, legal reports, analogous product
information, statistical data, government and private bodies' reports and market
trends' data.

A literature review has four main stages:

1. Issue(s)
what are the main issues under exploration? What are the relevant areas and what
are the associated component issues?

2. Literature search
searching and locating published materials relevant to the issue(s) under
exploration.

3. Literature evaluation
what are the key literature sources that will make a significant contribution to
understanding and addressing the issue(s) at hand?

4. Analysis and interpretation
what are the major findings and conclusions of the literature that has been deemed
relevant to the issue(s) under exploration?

It should be noted, however, that these stages may well be undertaken in an
iterative fashion and will not always necessarily be completed in the order
presented above. Careful attention should be placed on the evaluation, analysis
and interpretation of each piece of literature, and full consideration given to the
provenance of each article. What are the author's credentials? Are the author's
arguments supported by evidence (e.g. historical material, primary research, case
studies, statistics, scientific findings, etc.)? Each piece of literature under review
should have a certain degree of objectivity. Is the author's perspective even-
handed or prejudicial? Is opposing data presented or is certain relevant
information ignored to strengthen the points the author is making in his or her
paper? How persuasive is the author's writing? Which of the author's papers or
reports are the most or least convincing? Finally, and significantly, what is the value
of the literature that you have found and reviewed? Are the author's arguments
and conclusions convincing? Does the work contribute in any meaningful and
relevant way to the issue or exploration? Does it contribute a degree of knowledge
and/or understanding to the subject you are exploring?

Although a literature review itself does not present any new, primary
information, it is nevertheless a highly useful method for conducting research in
product design projects.

Internet searches

The internet has transformed society, putting vast amounts of data at our fingertips. Search engines allow us to conduct targeted searches for specific information, by typing in keywords that are run against a database of web pages. Internet searches typically involve users searching for information, but they might also provide navigational help (e.g. give you the URL of the website you want to reach) or transactional assistance (e.g. show you websites where you can perform a certain transaction, such as shop, download a file or locate a map). Today, there are hundreds of different web search tools, but 99.99 per cent of searches use Google, Yahoo!, MSN and Ask.com, in that order. Google is the biggest and most commonly used search engine on the planet, processing over 1 trillion unique URLs a day. But you should be aware that any search engine covers only a small fraction of all the pages on the internet, with even the major search engines indexing at best only about a third of documents available.

The sheer quantity of results provided by search engines can leave you feeling overwhelmed, but as long as you use the appropriate keywords, even a return of several thousand hits is not really a problem as search engines rank results by relevance. Different engines give different results and different relevance rankings, since some search all the text of a web page and/or document whereas others search only the first few sentences. By using a number of search engines you can cross-reference your searches, and begin to evaluate their value to you. When you find what you are looking for, do not take it at face value but try to check its authority – make sure the information is not inaccurate, unreliable, out of date, false or biased. The following questions will help you to evaluate the quality of any data:

Fig. 5
An example of an Internet search using the Google search engine. The internet has transformed the way design research is carried out nowadays, putting vast amounts of data at our fingertips.

— Does the information have a stated author or creator (whether personal or corporate) or is it anonymous?
— What is their educational or occupational background?
— Are they an unknown individual or someone connected with a respected professional association, educational institution or commercial publisher?
— Does the information seem to be accurate?
— Has the information been subjected to the rigours of peer and editorial review?
— When was the information last updated? Look for a date at the bottom of the page. Are any links to other websites still working?
— How objective is the information?
— Is it biased?
— Is the information promotional, i.e. is it commercial advertising or trying to sell you something?
— How comprehensive is the information?
— What kind of audience is it aimed at?
— Does that level match your requirements?

Fig. 6
It is a mistake to assume cultural groups are the same worldwide; the Western idea of the gloomy black-clad teenager doesn't necessarily translate to Japan, with its variety of subcultural groups who adapt the garish colours and styles of Japanese Manga and Anime.

Cultural comparisons

Globalization has forced designers to consider a diverse range of users and communities. When developing new products, designers must address the specific needs of these diverse audiences, and take into account the distinct sensibilities of users from different countries who speak different languages. Cultural comparisons are a research method that uses personal and/or published accounts to reveal differences in behaviours and artefacts between national or other cultural groups. This forensic approach helps designers to understand cultural factors and the implications for their designs when designing for unfamiliar or global markets.

Manufacturers increasingly tailor their products to the specific cultural requirements and tastes of different international markets. These variations can range from name and branding to size and colour. When Microsoft created the Xbox, for example, they designed two different sizes of controller, as human factors analysis by their design team had identified that Asian consumers had slightly smaller average hand sizes than American gamers. Different markets respond differently to the same product, so a product designed for western Europe may have to be modified for use in Japan.

Another example of different cultural sensibilities can be seen in the mobile phone sector. While the two-handed operation of the Blackberry smartphone has been broadly adopted by American users, the Japanese have been resistant to this type of mobile phone, preferring to purchase and use phones that enable one-handed typing functionality and use. User research by designers has identified that it is not so much that Japanese consumers like one-handed phones, but rather that there are environmental factors at play. These consumers often live in large urban conurbations and rely on public transport. One hand is often needed to grab a rail overhead on moving subway trains or buses to avoid falling over, leaving just one hand free to send text messages or surf the internet; as a result, Japanese consumers prefer smaller phones with all the keys within a thumb's reach.

Manufacturers will also target specific groups of young consumers, often defined by their tastes in fashion and music. These groups are commonly referred to as subcultures or 'urban tribes', and range from the Mods and Rockers of the 1960s to the Emos of today. Members of a subculture often signal their membership through a distinctive and symbolic use of style, which includes the adoption of symbolic products. These subcultures use products, garments and objects to help define themselves, with people only admitted to the group once they understand its codes, symbols and meanings. Designers try to decode the meanings assigned to products through learning how to read the cultural signs – a technique called semiotics, developed by French philosopher, Roland Barthes. Once the language has been understood, the subculture can be translated into products that appeal to a broader market. Using cultural comparisons, designers can develop products that recognize, reflect and respond to the different values and beliefs within different audiences and cultures, and the different perceptions and expectations they have of products.

Role playing

Role playing is a very flexible and effective way of gaining a better understanding of the key stakeholders involved in a project, and of raising important issues. By adopting roles such as clients, manufacturers and specialist end-users, designers can simulate the real-life experiences and activities that are demanded in particular contexts. For example, designers might role play specific situations, such as driving a taxi, serving cocktails in a bar or changing a wheel in a garage.

Role playing requires you to project future scenarios – a kind of 'what if'. In any particular future scenario, you are projecting yourself and others into an imaginary situation where you cannot completely control or predict the outcome, but you can anticipate some or all of the conditions and 'rehearse' your performance in order to shape the discussions and outcomes.

By adopting the roles of others, designers can gain valuable insights into what motivates certain stakeholders and what their objectives and values might be. Role play is defined generally as an experience around a specific situation that contains two or more different viewpoints or perspectives. The role play situation can be organized around a prepared brief and the different role perspectives on the same situation are handed out to the different people who will come together to discuss it. Each role has a particular objective, or set of objectives, they wish to achieve, which may well be in conflict with other role players.

Fig. 7
An example of role playing a situation in a hospital. Role playing is an effective way of gaining a deep understanding of particular situations and of raising important issues from different perspectives such as the clients, the manufacturers and specialist end-users.

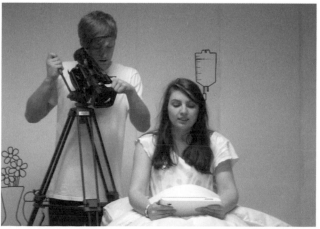

Role playing situations need to be realistic and relevant to the individuals playing the key roles; the most successful experiences focus carefully on developing particular situations and gaining knowledge and information from them. It is important to remember that role playing should be fun – it should not be a stressful experience for the people involved. It can help build design teams, develop employee motivation, improve communications and support excellent new product design and development. You should follow these simple guidelines to ensure you get the most out of role playing:

— Adequate preparation time is required – this might seem obvious, but it is often overlooked in the belief that it is best to get on with the role play quickly.

— Role playing must be focused – you must be clear at the outset about what you want people to achieve during the experience. Uncertain thinking at the outset will result in fuzzy outcomes. Clear thinking and preparation will result in clear and important outcomes.

— Role playing objectives must be clear and understood – if people are unclear about what they are supposed to do, your role play will be ineffective. The brief for everyone involved should be unambiguous: there should be clearly set objectives and enough information for people to engage in a believable and relevant conversation in line with these objectives. Be clear about the purpose of the role play situation, too. What information do you want to gain from conducting the session?

— Rehearse your role play – you will likely need to do it again and again to get it right. So you will need to rehearse again and again to get your behaviours and the role play relationships just right to make sense of the scene and understand the issues involved.

— Role playing ambitions – you need to be realistic in your ambitions for the role play. If you set your ambitions too high then you might cause people to lose confidence in themselves and in the role playing situation at hand. If you don't have time to get the participants to complete the whole exercise properly, in depth, with plenty of rehearsal and revisiting, then you may be better off completing just part of the situation.

— Role playing feedback – this is very important for achieving successful situations. Not only can the participants provide feedback on the roles they are playing, but they can also benefit from feedback from observers. Observers should explain their feedback clearly, following SMART principles (Specific, Measurable, Agreed, Realistic and Time-bound). Observers should describe the specific things that they saw and heard, relevant to the exercise and to the people doing the role playing. Role play feedback should avoid subjective judgements based on personal knowledge or assumptions. It should also provide meaningful and specific comments that the role players can act on.

Try it yourself

'Try it yourself' is a commonly used research method that enables designers to gain an appreciation of how a product, service or environment is experienced by actual users. Designers need to access people's experiences of products, actions and places, using the information as an invaluable source of inspiration. But how can you know how your product or service actually performs if you don't put yourself in the user's shoes? By actually using and experiencing a prototype, or an existing or new product, you can develop a deeper awareness of the multifaceted experiences that actual end-users encounter, as well as a greater understanding of a specific problem and/or activity.

        This method requires you to leave your studio and try the product/s as your real and/or target users do, and evaluate your proposed design. This might involve going out onto your local streets and purchasing a coffee and muffin in a local shopping centre, withdrawing or depositing cash in a city-centre ATM, or assembling flatpack furniture using only a series of hand tools. Through 'exploring by doing' you can experience the subtle differences between various design solutions, and gain insights that can inspire new design directions and opportunities.

        When employing this research method you should ensure that the experience is extensively recorded – keeping a detailed diary of photos and notes. 'Try it yourself' enables you to challenge your preconceptions and provides an opportunity for you to reflect critically upon what you are trying to achieve.

Fig. 8
By putting yourself in the user's shoes, you can develop a better understanding of the issues that your customers will face, rather than merely looking at the product from a design perspective.

Mind mapping

A mind map is a visual representation of hierarchical information. Mind mapping, made popular by the psychologist Tony Buzan in his 1974 book *Use Your Head*, is a great method for creating visual representations of words and ideas. It is said to improve memory and develop deeper thought processes by encouraging greater use of the right lobe of the brain (responsible for creativity and intuition), balancing out the use of the left and right lobes. Designers can make good use of mind mapping during the early stages of design projects, particularly when problem solving and generating concept proposals.

Mind maps help you to think and learn better. They help you solve problems creatively and enable you to take action. Mind maps encourage creativity and flexibility, and they help you think outside the box. A mind map can be used to represent an entire concept or an idea with branches of associated thoughts. As with other visual learning techniques, mind maps provide a simplified overview of complex information, allowing a user to understand relationships better and to find new connections.

Mind maps help you to avoid overly linear thinking, which is why they are so useful for designers. They are arguably more appropriate than lists or bullet points, since most design problems are not linear and orderly by nature. They include a central idea or image surrounded by branches of associated topics or ideas. Subtopics are then added to the branches as ideas flow freely. Typically in a mind map, the topic and subtopic text is one to two keywords, to provide a reminder for what the idea is; more information is then detailed in attached notes. Mind mapping is a commonly used for brainstorming and note taking. The process of building a mind map is very fluid and non-linear, making the expansion of ideas similar to the natural way of thinking. Symbols and images, along with keywords, are used to retain and recall information quickly. Branches and their associations are often created in different colours to help with identification and memory.

Another popular diagrammatic research method is concept mapping, developed by Professor Joseph D. Novak at Cornell University in the 1960s. As with mind mapping, this graphically illustrates relationships between information. In a concept map, two or more concepts are linked by words that describe their relationship. Concept maps encourage understanding by helping designers to organize and enhance their knowledge on any topic – designers learn new information by integrating each new idea into their existing body of knowledge. The use of both mind map and concept map techniques is widespread in the design industry. Imagination and association are the keys to high-level memory and creative thinking and both forms of mapping support this. Since many designers are visual or kinaesthetic learners, these visual approaches enable them to structure, present and evaluate research findings in an effective and successful manner.

Fig. 9
This 'word cloud' has been generated by the application Wordle™, which gives greater prominence to words that appear more frequently in the source text (here taken from the opposite page); it creates a hierarchy and allows us to visualize the key points.

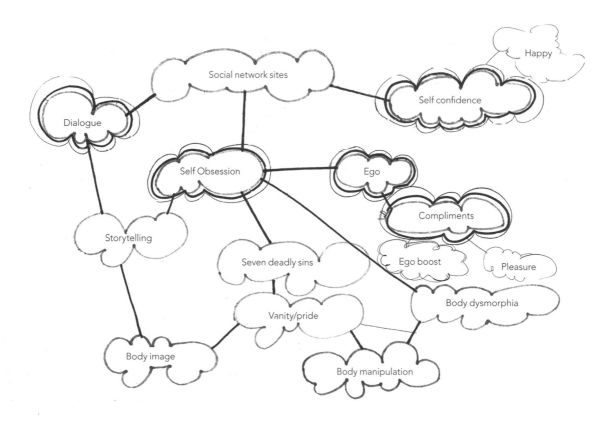

Fig. 10
A simple mind map showing how words and ideas are generated around a central theme.

Sampling

The key aim behind sampling is to gain knowledge and information from a subset of individuals from within a population that can then be used to describe the whole population. A population is a group of individuals, objects or items from which samples are taken for measurement. For example, designers might be interested in a population of car owners or mobile phone users, electronic book readers or university students.

Designers will never be in a position to survey very large populations for two fundamental reasons. First, the costs involved in carrying out very large surveys can be extremely high. Second, populations are dynamic, in that the individuals making up the population change over time. Sampling, therefore, provides several advantages:

1. Costs can be kept low.
2. Data collection can be conducted faster.
3. Since the data set (i.e. sample) is smaller, it is possible to ensure high quality and accurate data.

A sample is expected to represent the population from which it comes. However, there is never a guarantee that any sample will accurately denote this population; there is always the possibility that the sample of people that have been interviewed, for example, are unrepresentative of the population. This is usually because of a sampling error. For example, 100 college design students are measured and are all found to be over 1.9 metres tall. It is obvious that this would be a highly unrepresentative sample that would inevitably lead to invalid conclusions. This is an unlikely occurrence because naturally these cases (i.e. college design students over 1.9 metres tall) would be distributed more widely

Fig. 11
Sampling is used to gain information from a group of individuals from within a specific population that can then be used to describe the whole population. For example, a sample might be shoppers in a particular area of Japan, such as this precinct in Tokyo.

among the population. However, these and other types of sampling errors can occur. There are several methods of sampling to choose from.
Simple random sampling is perhaps the easiest and most ideal, but designers can also utilize the following:

— **Probability methods** e.g. simple random sampling, stratified sampling, systematic sampling and cluster sampling. This is the best overall group of sampling methods to use if you require statistical analyses on the data you collect.

— **Quota methods** e.g. quota sampling, proportionate quota sampling and non-proportionate quota sampling. Quota methods are appropriate when you can determine the number of people you need to sample. For example, when you are studying a number of groups you will need equivalent numbers to enable subsequent equivalent analyses and conclusions.

— **Selective methods** e.g. purposive or behaviour sampling, expert sampling, snowball sampling, modal instance sampling and diversity sampling. Selective methods are best if you are focusing on particular groups of the population. For example, observing how a group of working mothers uses their mobile phones in a specific context.

— **Convenience methods** e.g. snowball sampling, convenience sampling and judgement sampling. These methods are useful when you are unable to access a wider population due to time or cost constraints.

— **Ethnographic methods** e.g. selective sampling, theoretical sampling, convenience sampling and judgement sampling. If you are using one of these methods you will need to use your own judgement to select what seems like an appropriate sample.

Significant savings in design projects can be made if an appropriate sampling method is used, an appropriate sample size is selected and necessary precautions are taken to reduce sampling and measurement errors. Furthermore, the selection and use of an appropriate sample method should deliver valid and reliable information.

Case Study

Bill Gaver's Cultural Probes

Introduction

Cultural probes are evocative tasks given to people to elicit inspiring material for design. They are usually used at the outset of projects to help find out about relevant people and situations.

Objective

Rather than helping to develop an objective account of those subjects, however, cultural probes anticipate and provoke more personal, idiosyncratic and partial encounters. Probes often take the form of a collection of distinct but related items that address a variety of themes via different media, such as cameras, drawing tasks and materials requesting written responses.

Methods

Bill Gaver is Professor of Design at Goldsmiths in London, where he also heads the Interaction Research Studio. Gaver first developed the cultural probes user research technique together with Tony Dunne and Elena Pacenti for their EU-funded Presence Project. The probes for this project used a collection of maps, postcards, cameras and photo albums with various requests for participants to reveal themselves. In a later project on the home called Equator, a new team that included Gaver, Andy Boucher, Sarah Pennington and Brendan Walker extended the repertoire to include more unusual items, such as a request to diagram relationships with friends or family using graphics of a seaside, or a

cricket game, or Dante's heaven and hell; a drinking glass for listening and describing interesting sounds around the home; and a device for recording a short account of a recent dream.

Another project, with France Telecom, concerned caravaners, so Nadine Jarvis and Andy Boucher put together a collection of materials that included supplies for making snow globe souvenirs of the journey, a journal for noting night-time sounds and a kit for mapping caravan parks.

In each of these examples, the probes were characterized by multiple items, each addressing different issues and using different media, and each open-ended – or even absurd – to encourage participants to reveal their lives in rich and engaging ways. At heart, though, probes are defined by an attitude towards user research, not a set of typical forms. They reflect not only these designers' doubts that user research can ever fully uncover the experiences of other people, but also their unwillingness to do so, lest their imagination as designers becomes overwhelmed by participants' desires.

Cultural probes embody a sense of play that seems invaluable in design, a willingness to entertain unusual or even contradictory ideas, to accept ambiguity and to engage with the world with seriousness and humour simultaneously. The form through which this attitude is expressed is secondary. So, for instance, in a recent study Gaver's team worked with the illustrator Alexandra Antonopoulou to create a

'storybook probe', in which participants were asked to fill in the gaps in a story about waking up to find that they were 'the size of a pea'.

Results

What is important about probes is that they are risky. They pose questions and set up situations that are uncontrolled and unpredictable, because they are designed to provide surprising new views into people's lives, not confirmation of pre-existing opinions. If the glimpses they offer are fragmentary and impossible to analyze, then so much the better – in this way they help remind designers that understanding the situations for which they design is an ongoing process that is always provisional, and never really concluded.

Above: Selection of cultural probes (from l
eft to right, top to bottom) Listening Glass from
the Equator Project; Dream Recorder from the
Equator Project; Snow Ball Souvenir Kit from
the France Telecom Project; Night Sound from the
France Telecom Project; two Story Book probes.

Case Study

Adidas
ClimaCool Trainer

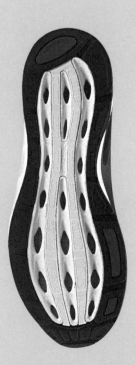

Introduction

Adidas launched their first ClimaCool running shoe in 2001. It was the first trainer on the market to be designed with 360 degrees of ventilation and redefined how a running shoe could look and feel. Ben Herath, Design Director of Running Footwear, was tasked with creating the 2012 reincarnation of the ClimaCool trainer.

Objective

The objective was to create a highly ventilated trainer that would also provoke a new visual language around the company's Clima Technology on its ten-year anniversary.

Methods

The designers began by studying the 2001 ClimaCool trainer, and focused on enhancing its ventilation properties – the more a runner can control his or her temperature, the more comfortable they will be. Research showed that the foot heats up most along the foot bed and in the mid-foot area, so the new design focused on making these hot zones highly ventilated. Holes were opened up along the midsole to allow air underneath the foot, and moisture-wicking materials were applied in high sweat areas.

Adidas studied groups of consumers and found that ClimaCool technology resonated with spring and summer time, when many travellers want a fun, colourful running shoe for their holidays. This prompted the idea of a shoe with cooling vents that allowed it to breathe and exhale. The company wanted to communicate this benefit in a highly visual, fun way, so they analyzed every part of the shoe, from outside to inside, from tooling to upper, pushing the boundaries of how much material could be removed while still allowing the shoe to perform as a running shoe. They perforated, punched holes, drilled and cut material away.

Adidas adopted a biological form of competitor method analysis and looked to precedents in nature for inspiration. (Nature is constantly shedding material it doesn't need, and continuously cutting holes in things.) This resulted in organic shapes that looked like they had been created by wind. The new ClimaCool trainer has been designed with a PU (polyurethane) comfort midsole and a new upper layering system. PU provides a very cushioned, comfortable feel and it allowed Adidas to create holes throughout the midsole in nearly every direction. For the upper textiles, a new three-layer construction was adopted: the base layer has wicking properties to help control moisture within the shoe, the middle layer is a minimal skeletal layer that supports the foot, and the top layer is a micro-fine monofilament layer that allows air through.

Results

The nature-inspired minimal upper construction traces air circulation lines around the foot; the material package is translucent, so the minimal structure guides the eye along the same path that air might circulate around the foot. As the mid-foot is one of the hottest areas, the Adidas signature three stripes were moved so they didn't block air. This resulted in a new, unexpected placement for the iconic logo.

How to write a literature review

Conducting a comprehensive literature review requires you to follow, step-by-step, a series of important stages:

1. Problem formulation

What is the main problem you are attempting to resolve? Are there any relevant or associated problems? What subjects and/or disciplines have data, information and/or knowledge that might help resolve the main problem and any associated problems and issues? For example, the root of the problem might be an 'energy' issue, and physical scientists and/or engineers may possess relevant information and knowledge. However, you might need to delve deeper to find the information and knowledge you require from more specific scientists and/or engineers, such as geologists, material scientists, mechanical engineers and electronic engineers, for example. You should always have an open mind on the data and information you collect and seek to find competing and opposing data. Are the 'experts' always correct? Is there another way? Why is information from source A so different to that from source B?

2. Data collection

Where will you find the data, information and knowledge that you need to help you undertake the design project? How will you collect it? How wide and deep will you search for it? You need to ensure that you cover as wide a review of the literature as you possibly can in the time permitting, including published articles, papers, books, reports, academic dissertations, conference papers, trade magazine articles, patent searches, legal reports, analagous product information, statistical data, government and private bodies' reports and market trends' data. All of these would be relevant in a typical product design project.

3. Data evaluation

How will you evaluate the data and information that you collect and review? What criteria will you use for this evaluation? For example, what is the provenance of the information – that is, how authentic is it and what is its quality? Is the report objective? Has the author been unbiased or prejudicial in his or her reporting of the research? How persuasive is the report? What is the value of the data and information that you have found and reviewed?

4. Analysis and interpretation

What are the major findings and/or recommendations of the literature that you have reviewed? What will be the focus of your analysis? Will the analysis be based on quantitative or qualitative data, or both? The analysis and interpretation of the data and information that you have collected during your literature search is an important element of the literature review and should help you structure your report and presentation for the next stage.

5. Literature review presentation

You need to ensure that you cover the literature you have reviewed as comprehensively as possible in your presentation. So, as a guide, your presentation should include a rich overview of the subject, issue or problem under consideration, along with the objectives of the literature review. You should then divide the work you have found in your review into categories (e.g. those in support of a particular position, those against and those offering completely different positions entirely), showing how each work is similar to or different from the others.

Literature review

1. Changing times
1.1 Fast fashion
    1.1.1 true cost of fast fashion
1.2 Growth of the value sector
1.3 The high street
1.4 The ethical consumer
1.5 The fashion industry
1.6 Impact of the recession

2. Defining ethical

3. The ethical fashion market
3.1 Market segmentation
3.2 High street availability
3.3 Labelling

4. Consumer purchasing behaviour
4.1 Ethical awareness levels
4.2 Influential factors
4.3 Justification strategies
4.4 Purchasing hierarchy
4.5 The intention – behaviour gap
4.6 The purchasing process

5. The role of the retailer
5.1 Corporate social responsibility (CSR)
5.2 Who controls the industry
5.3 Retailer/consumer communication

6. Conclusions

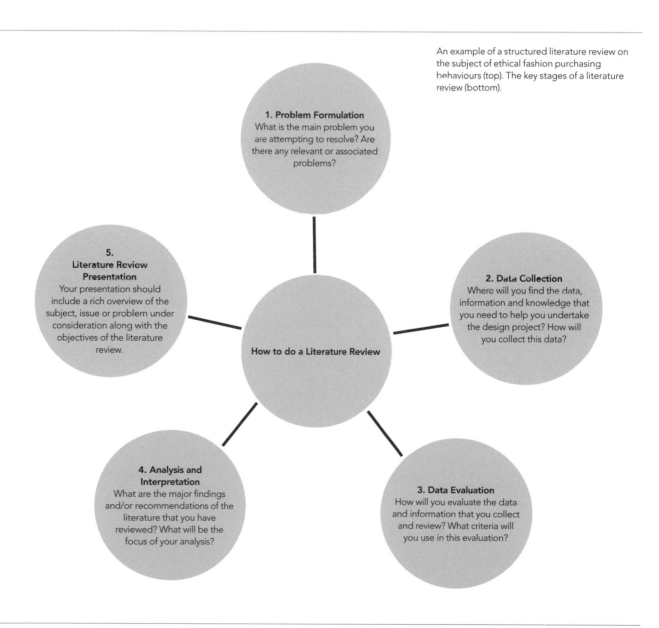

An example of a structured literature review on the subject of ethical fashion purchasing behaviours (top). The key stages of a literature review (bottom).

1. Problem Formulation
What is the main problem you are attempting to resolve? Are there any relevant or associated problems?

2. Data Collection
Where will you find the data, information and knowledge that you need to help you undertake the design project? How will you collect this data?

3. Data Evaluation
How will you evaluate the data and information that you collect and review? What criteria will you use in this evaluation?

4. Analysis and Interpretation
What are the major findings and/or recommendations of the literature that you have reviewed? What will be the focus of your analysis?

5. Literature Review Presentation
Your presentation should include a rich overview of the subject, issue or problem under consideration along with the objectives of the literature review.

How to do a Literature Review

How to create a
great mind map

To create a great mind map you will need only the most basic of tools – a sheet of paper and a set of different coloured pens or pencils. Most people find it easier to turn the page on its side and complete their mind map in 'landscape' format – this gives the maximum space for ideas to radiate out from the centre. Begin by writing or sketching an image of the main issue in the middle of the page. This can be as simple as a succinct phrase contained within a box or circle.

Next, think up new ideas, action points and statements that relate to the main word(s) or phrase and radiate these out from the central idea. Each new idea should be contained within a box or circle of its own and connected by a line extending in any direction from the main image. You could use a range of different colours so that related ideas and issues are grouped together. The colours you select are not important, but some emphasis should be placed on producing a visually rich and appealing mind map that will interest and stimulate others. You can also enhance your mind map by using different line thicknesses for your branches, arrows, groups, colours and shapes. This process should be repeated as many times as is required to create a number of sub-issues and sub-topics.

The completed mind map may be simple, with just two or three sub-topics, or it may be a complex mind map comprising tens or hundreds of ideas, sub-ideas, topics, sub-topics and connecting lines. You need to focus on the key ideas, using your own words, and then look for connections between words, ideas and issues. The visual mind mapping method helps both your creativity and your memory. It will help you to understand and recall

information better, be open to more possibilities, and avoid the restrictions inherent in a list format.

You should work quickly without pausing to judge what you have written or drawn. Do not edit. Tinkering and working slowly will allow linear thinking and 'analysis paralysis' to set in. Pausing and judging the mind map that you are creating also disrupts the process, which can have negative results. You must avoid the notion that things have to be perfect before you can begin. The key is to think creatively in a non-linear way, working quickly and without worrying about whether everything is correct, appropriate or neat and tidy. So, in order to create a great mind map, use these simple-to-follow guidelines:

— Write down the central idea or use a central multicoloured image that signifies the mind map subject.
— Think up new ideas related to the central idea.
— Use themes to provide the main divisions of the mind map.
— Enclose each theme with an outline that hugs the shape created by the branches.
— Make sure that the lines that support each key word are the same length as the word and 'organically' connect to the central image.
— Print so that each word used is clear and legible.
— Try to use single key words uncluttered by adjectives or definitions.
— Use colour for vividness and to enhance memory recollection.

Detailed mind map looking at the motivations and considerations surrounding the central theme of travel.

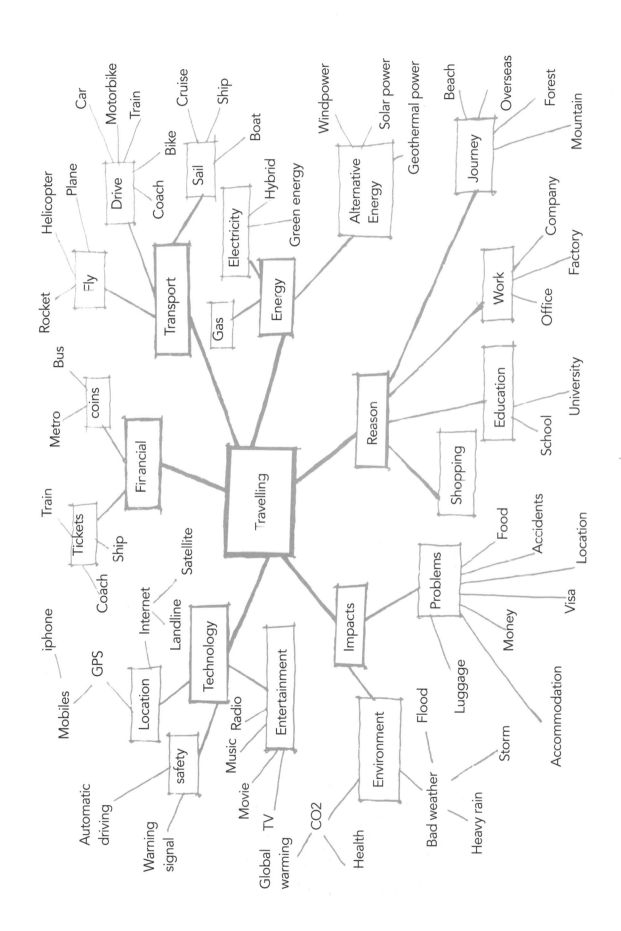

Transport
- Fly — Rocket, Helicopter, Plane
- Drive — Car, Motorbike, Train, Bike, Coach
- Sail — Cruise, Ship, Boat

Energy
- Electricity — Hybrid, Green energy
- Gas
- Alternative Energy — Windpower, Solar power, Geothermal power

Journey — Beach, Overseas, Forest, Mountain

Financial
- coins — Bus, Metro
- Tickets — Train, Ship, Coach

Technology
- Location — Internet, Landline, Satellite
  - GPS — iphone, Mobiles
  - safety — Automatic driving, Warning signal
- Entertainment — Music, Radio, Movie, TV

Travelling (central)

Reason
- Work — Company, Factory, Office
- Education — School, University
- Shopping

Impacts
- Environment — Flood, CO2, Global warming, Health

Problems — Food, Accidents, Location, Visa, Money, Luggage, Storm, Accommodation, Bad weather, Heavy rain

ASKING

Designers can enlist the participation of people in the design process through a range of design research methods that pose questions to help reveal and discover information that can prove invaluable in resolving complex design issues. One of the simplest and quickest ways of eliciting information from individuals is by asking them directly. Using tools and techniques such as questionnaires, focus groups, interviews and the creation of personas, designers can gain a better understanding of the multifaceted relationships that exist between users and the designed products, services and systems they rely on.

Questionnaires and surveys

The words 'questionnaire' and 'survey' are often used interchangeably and confusion can sometimes arise. Questionnaires, however, are basically a printed list of questions, whereas a survey encompasses a range of different elements, including a sample design, a data collection methodology, data collection instruments, analytic techniques, etc. A questionnaire is only one type of data collection instrument. Generally speaking, questions should be clearly stated and there should be a logical flow from one question to the next. To achieve the best response rates, questions should flow from the least sensitive to the most sensitive and from the general to the specific.

Questionnaires and surveys are a relatively simple yet effective way of obtaining information from people. However, one major disadvantage of written questionnaires is the possibility of low response rates. Questionnaires posted out have a response rate of only around one in four returns, although this rate increases when other media formats and approaches are employed. Another disadvantage of questionnaires is the inability to probe responses and, when nearly 90 per cent of all communication between one individual and another is visual, gestures and other visual cues are potentially lost.

This method can be useful, however, for ascertaining particular traits and values of many users relatively quickly. Questionnaires and surveys can be conducted via email, the internet, by post, by telephone and by researchers asking people for responses on the street, in their workplace or at home. Online surveys have had a significant impact on how researchers undertake research. Manufacturers' websites increasingly use devices such as pop-ups and banner surveys to engage people browsing their sites and gather responses, comments

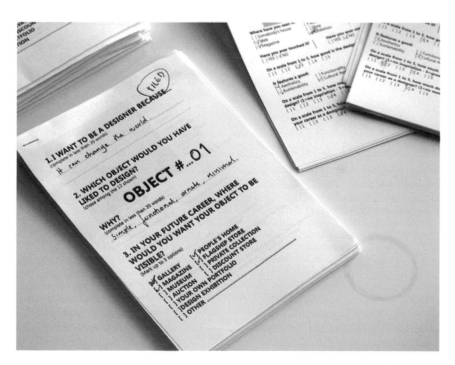

Fig. 1
Example of a printed questionnaire with multiple-option answers to help structure the results.

and data from a far broader range of potential customers. There are a number of easy-to-use, customizable templates you can use to construct a questionnaire or survey online, and conduct your own research within minutes.

There are two main types of questionnaire – fixed-response questionnaires and open-ended questionnaires. Fixed-response questionnaires are ones that present a number of alternative responses to a question. Users are asked to mark the option they feel is most appropriate, or rate the options on a sliding scale, perhaps from 1 'strongly agree', through 2 'agree', 3 'not sure', 4 'disagree' to 5 'strongly disagree'.

Open-ended questionnaires ask the respondent to write down their own answers to questions, such as 'What do you like about your bicycle?' or 'Can you suggest things that would improve your bicycle's performance?'. Open-ended questionnaires are therefore particularly useful during the early stages of the design process, when the design team might not be entirely sure of the important issues associated with the product being developed.

Focus and unfocus groups

A focus group consists of a number of people brought together in one place to discuss a particular issue or set of issues. The discussions may deal with particular aspects of a designed product, service or system, such as the users' experiences of using a vacuum cleaner, for example. Or they can be more general discussions, exploring, for example, the range of contexts users encounter when using cleaning products in the home. Usually the participants will meet face to face, but focus groups held between people located in different places over large geographical distances using video conferencing are also increasingly common these days.

Focus groups are a form of group interview that capitalizes on the communication between participants to generate information. Although group interviews are often used as a quick and convenient way to collect information from several people simultaneously, focus groups explicitly use group interaction

Fig. 2
A focus group on the topic of 'medical care'. Participants are role playing.

as part of the method. Focus groups typically involve around 8 to 12 individuals who are led by a moderator for anything up to two hours in duration. The group works to a loosely structured agenda, which is an effective way to generate ideas and develop understanding on particular themes without having to reach consensus. The aim is to allow the participants to take the lead in determining the direction of the discussions, while the moderator simply ensures that all the members of the group are able to voice their opinions.

The moderator should also create a set of prompts in case the session loses direction. These prompts should simply be a means of generating further conversation; they should be carefully designed so that they do not lead the participants into giving particular responses. For example, an inappropriate prompt would be 'Don't you find that this handle is difficult to grip?'. A more productive prompt would be 'How easy or difficult do you find this handle to grip?'. The first prompt is a leading question, while the second is stated in a neutral way.

An unfocus group is a useful method for gaining a number of diverse and sometimes opposing or conflicting interpretations on a given design problem. An unfocus group involves a diverse group of individuals in a workshop-style setting contributing to concept design generation or evaluation activities. Unfocus groups encourage rich, creative and diverse insights which may open up new areas of design activity.

User narration

User narration, sometimes referred to as 'think aloud protocols', is a valuable method for identifying users' concerns, desires and motivations when using specific products, systems and services. It involves asking users to think about and describe aloud their experience as they perform a specific activity or operate a product in a particular context. Running a good user narration session relies on having something for the participants to interact with, so the organizers should provide an interactive prototype of the designed product, service or system being proposed. Alternatively, the session organizers might wish to utilize existing, competing products that the participants can use and narrate.

Users might be asked to perform specific tasks in a particular order, or asked to explore the product, service or system freely. Giving users set tasks to follow in a predetermined order is useful for uncovering specific issues, whereas user narration in free exploration mode can reveal information on why users use some features of a product and ignore others. During a session the investigator will usually prompt participants to verbalize their thoughts. The prompts might be along the lines of 'What are you thinking of now?'. Or they may be more specific and relate to a particular issue or design feature, such as 'Why did you press that button at that time?'. Users' narrations can also provide valuable emotional responses to products, which can be prompted by questions such as 'How do you feel when you use the product?'.

User narration is an excellent method for understanding not only what problems users have with designed products, services and systems, but also why these problems arise. User narration sessions with small numbers of participants can provide rich data that can lead to better design solutions. One possible disadvantage of this method, however, is the risk of interference between a user's verbalizations, the tasks they are performing with the product and their interaction with the investigator. For example, too much prompting by the investigator can lead to the user making things up in order to be seen to be providing feedback; too little can lead to the user providing less data than might otherwise be the case. Prompting needs to be done in a skilful, careful and balanced way.

Fig. 3
Users 'thinking aloud' while using an interactive product, allowing researchers to understand their concerns and motivations.

Interviews

One of the simplest ways to explore whether or not users are happy with a product, service or system is to ask them. Interviews basically comprise a series of questions, which are posed directly to the participants. When interviewing users, for example, product designers can ask how they feel when using the product, whether it is easy or difficult to operate, whether they enjoy using it or find it frustrating or annoying. There are three broad categories of interviews that a designer can draw upon – unstructured, semi-structured and structured.

In an unstructured interview the investigator will typically ask each respondent a series of open-ended questions. This gives the respondents opportunities to direct the discussion towards issues that they consider the most important rather than sticking to a predetermined list of questions drawn up by the interviewer. An unstructured interview is an appropriate approach to take, therefore, in situations where the interviewer doesn't know beforehand what the main issues of those being interviewed are likely to be.

In a semi-structured interview, the person asking the questions will usually have a better idea of the main issues surrounding the design project and the questions they wish to ask the respondent. Semi-structured interviews are, by their very nature, a little more constrained than unstructured interviews. The interviewer will usually use prompts to ensure that the specific areas and points they want to cover are addressed, while still allowing for some unstructured contributions from the interviewee.

Fig. 4
Interviews are basically a series of questions posed directly to the participants. Below, architect Rory Hyde interviews designer Ross Lovegrove at the Venice Biennale. On the right, designer Marco Merendi being interviewed at the Cersai fair stand of Rapsel by a H.O.M.E. journalist.

Structured interviews ask respondents to select responses from a predetermined list. For example, an interviewee might be asked to rank features of a new product's aesthetic value on a five-point scale, where 5 means high aesthetic value and 1 means low aesthetic value. This sort of psychometric scale is a device invented by the American psychologist, Rensis Lickert. Interviewee responses in structured interviews provide data that can be analyzed quantitatively, but the issues relating to the product being designed need to be known and well understood beforehand.

Interviews are a flexible method that can be used at various stages of the design process – from helping to formulate specific aspects of the brief and helping to select potential concept ideas through to using prototypes and sharing users' opinions and insights. Interviews eliminate the possibility of misinterpretation between the investigator and the respondent as they usually take place face to face, which is not always the case with questionnaires and surveys, for example.

Be your customer/client

This research method sees the researcher become a consumer in an attempt to actually experience and understand first-hand what real customers feel. It involves leaving the design studio and actually experiencing the entire customer cycle, from evaluating to buying to owning and using the product that you currently design/produce. It enables you to determine which touchpoints deliver a positive experience, and which can be improved.

When undertaking this form of research, designers often take on the role of a mystery shopper. Market research agencies, consumer watchdog organizations and companies use this technique to measure criteria such as quality of service or regulatory compliance, or to gather specific information about their own or competitors' products and services. While gathering information, researchers usually do not declare their activities – they perform their research 'undercover', which can pose ethical issues. Mystery shoppers may sometimes be required to take photographs or measurements, return purchases to evaluate customer service procedures, or record quantitative data such as the number of sales, or the time taken to be served by staff.

Research tools for typical 'Be your customer' assessments range from simple questionnaires to comprehensive video recordings. Researchers often complement these field studies by testing the knowledge and service skills of those representing a product, brand or service by asking atypical questions or posing specific challenges to evaluate a range of scenarios. Research data can then be reviewed and analyzed to provide quantitative and qualitative statistical analysis reports, helping the design team and company as a whole to design better products, services and customer experiences.

By asking your company or client to describe or enact their typical customer's experience, and then comparing this to the 'Be your customer' research findings, you can highlight any reality gaps between a company's internal perception of itself, its offerings and its customers, and those held by its actual customers. You can also undertake stakeholder workshops, where working with existing and/or prospective customers can help identify problems and potential solutions.

When developing a new product or merely refining an existing one, it is vital to challenge your assumptions and place yourself in the shoes of your users. Ask questions, such as 'What value would this new product bring to a prospective buyer?', 'What price would they consider reasonable?' and 'What reasons might they have for not buying?'. By becoming your customer, you can fully evaluate a product, from the retail experience of purchasing it, through to use and aftersales support, and thereby generate invaluable detailed data and feedback.

Fig. 5
The design researcher adopting the role of 'Be your Customer'. This method allows the researcher to experience and understand first-hand what customers experience during the entire consumer cycle, from buying to owning and using the product, service or system in question.

Fig. 6
Selection of leading global brands' logos.

Brand DNA analysis

The branded products we use and consume say a great deal about our individual tastes and personalities. A brand is an amalgam of product design, logos, slogans, advertising, marketing, packaging and consumer recognition. Designers need to ensure that their products inspire an emotional resonance in consumers, encouraging them to develop a relationship with a brand or product line that evolves over a lifetime of purchasing. As consumers we embrace brands because we feel we are getting more than just a physical product, and we choose from a nuanced family of products that evolve to meet our needs, wants and desires over time. Brands promote consumer choice, and through the development of brand 'extensions', manufacturers are able to target a range of consumers.

Consumers are drawn to branded products because they embody values they are attracted to – such as authenticity or exclusivity – and a range of research techniques have developed over the years to help designers cater for consumers who wish to position themselves socially through the products they purchase.

Brand DNA analysis is a holistic method that aims to reveal the multilayered aspects of a branded product through the integration of data gathered from questionnaires, focus groups and detailed formal design analysis. The technique evaluates a product through a range of perspectives:

Aesthetics
Sensorial perspective. How does the product look, feel, smell and sound?

Interaction
Behavioural perspective. How do users interact with the product? What behaviours does the product encourage?

Performance
Functional perspective. What does a product do? What problems does it solve?

Construction
Physical perspective. How is the product made? What is it made of? What technologies does it employ?

Meaning
Mental perspective. What meanings and emotions does the product provoke?

Brand DNA analysis explores the design language, visual codes and signifiers that embody a brand, and how a brand's values are translated into a physical design. Products are complex, multilayered creations that communicate to consumers on a number of levels, and brand DNA analysis helps ensure that a product genuinely works within the context of its market competitors, while also conforming to the brand identity of its parent company/manufacturer. Brand DNA analysis can also be used to remodel an existing brand strategy.

Brandscaping
This form of analysis reveals which product is the most representative of a brand, what its most characteristic elements are, and which features are the most important for each design layer. This information can then be used to compare and contrast your product and brand against its rivals through a structured evaluation of a sector – known as brandscaping.

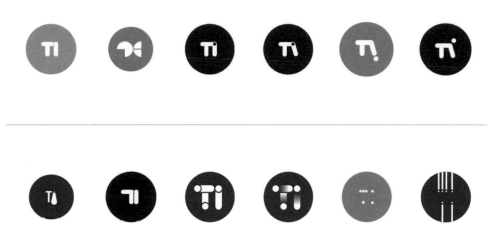

A typical analysis will determine the guiding principles and rules of a brand as seen by consumers from across the target global markets. It will reveal what consumers think about the look, feel and impression generated by a brand's logo, products, retail environments, advertising, marketing and customer service. Such specific cultural and market data is invaluable when determining the future direction of a brand, and drawing up local, regional and/or global brand guidelines – the documents produced by companies to assure the consistent tone and use of brand values and identity.

Brand DNA is an ongoing research process. Brands are living entities, and design researchers need to be continually monitoring the evolving consumer attitudes to ensure that a brand's products and proposition respond to these cultural changes while remaining true to the brand's core values.

Fig. 7
Brand development of three logos developed around the name 'Tangible Interactions', created to meet a number of different markets.

Market and retail research

Market research is the observation of how rival products are advertised, fitted into the market context and retailed in order to discover how the product field is merchandised overall. Researchers aim to uncover the immediate 'brandscape' of competitive brands surrounding a product and establish what the overall visual impression of the sector is.

Retail research studies how people shop in a particular sector, and how much time they devote to browsing. What elements of the 'design language' in this marketplace seem to be the critical ones used by the consumers in making brand choices? Is this a market balanced between buyers and users – for example, a sector featuring adults buying for children? And does this product sector seem to represent an 'easy buy' for consumers, or do they find it confusing or difficult? Commonly used market and retail research techniques include:

Product camouflage

This method involves designers modifying a series of existing designs, each with different elements removed. The designers then use a focus group to discuss the saliency of different visual elements. The disappearance of some elements may cause the perception of a product to alter.

Name swapping

Another popular technique, this involves swapping the names and logos on different product designs from the same market, and then discussing if and why the resulting designs are 'wrong' for the branded products being researched.

Fig. 8
Research board by Tom Harper, examining the market place and uses for domestic cleaning products.

Drawing from memory

This method reveals the most memorable features of a particular product or sector. Consumers are handed blank paper and are asked to draw particular products from memory. This is followed by an in-depth discussion with the group about what each of them has drawn and why.

Touchpoint analysis

Customers experience a product in many different ways, both directly and indirectly. The means by which customers come into contact with a product, brand or service throughout its lifecycle are called 'touchpoints'. Touchpoint analysis is a research technique that breaks these points down into three distinct areas of investigation:

— pre-purchase (marketing and advertising),
— purchase (retail) and
— post-purchase (product use and after-sales care).

A commonly used tool for evaluating the entire customer journey is the touchpoint wheel, which summarizes all the points of interaction where a customer can be intentionally/unintentionally influenced. The benefits of using touchpoint analysis can include better value for the consumer, greater brand loyalty and an increase in profitability for the retailer.

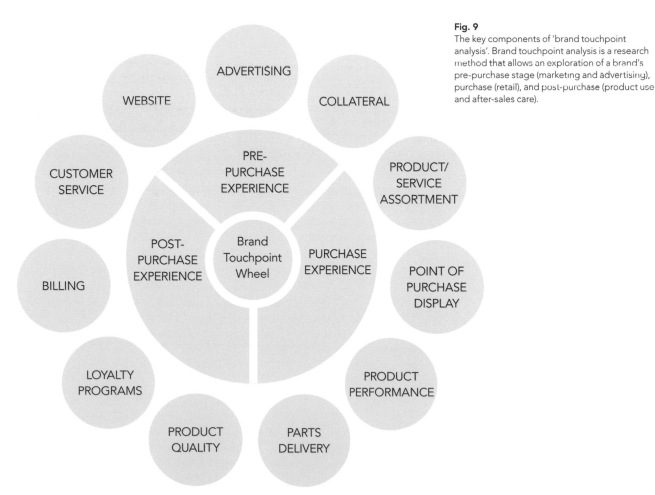

Fig. 9
The key components of 'brand touchpoint analysis'. Brand touchpoint analysis is a research method that allows an exploration of a brand's pre-purchase stage (marketing and advertising), purchase (retail), and post-purchase (product use and after-sales care).

Fig. 10
Inspiration board by designer Rosie MacCurrach for her 'Tales from the Land' collection.

Fig. 11
(Opposite, top) Pantone View Colour Planner contains inspirational photographs and matching colour chips, and forecasts new directions in colour trends.

Fig. 12
(Opposite, middle and bottom) Pages from Andrea Dall'Olios's SS 2010 *Home Interior Trend* book, complete with tactile fabric swatches.

Image and mood boards

Image or mood boards are loosely structured collaged boards that are widely used by designers to portray a range of potential directions for a specific product and/or brand intended for the marketplace. It is important to go beyond the obvious, yet keep the boards credible in the context of the product and brand. Image or mood boards are typically used in conjunction with 2D and 3D drawings and models. They are employed by designers to convey the overall feeling of a project, and involve placing a collection of carefully selected images and objects together on a series of A2- or A3-sized presentation boards which are intended to inspire, target particular desires and facilitate creativity and innovation. They may use photos, illustrations, magazine cut-outs, sample materials and so on to highlight the colour options, typographic possibilities, and the general look and feel of the product, service or system being proposed.

Image and mood boards are also very useful at the early stages of a design project: they can communicate the subjective and emotional aspects of a design to a client and secure their approval before proceeding further. They can also provide designers with feedback before too much time is invested. There is no set formula to creating a successful image or mood board, and they are often intentionally casual. However, carefully taking the client's list of experience characteristics and ideal features into consideration will help to create boards that are appropriate and effective.

Image and mood boards engage stakeholders by facilitating rich discussion and participation between the design team, clients and end-users, particularly during the early stages of the design process. Time dedicated to creating boards at the outset of a project can save time later on in the process. Thus, image and mood boards can be a more cost-effective and efficient way of illustrating a number of design possibilities than other alternative techniques.

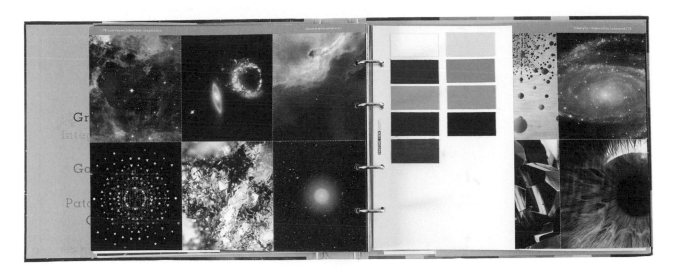

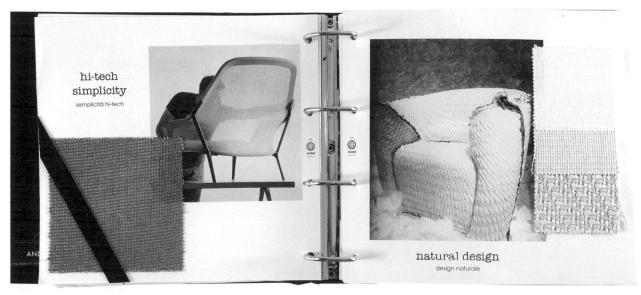

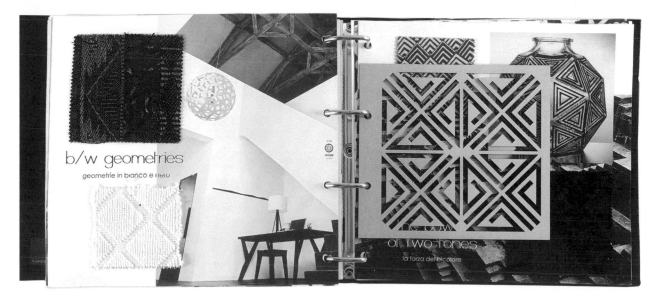

Perceptual mapping

When developing a new brand or product line a company needs to select its target market, and then decide how it wants to position its offering(s) within their chosen market segment, or brandscape. This activity is called market positioning and addresses how organizations want their consumers to see their product. Developing a positioning strategy depends on how competitors position themselves. A company needs to decide whether it wants to develop a 'me too' strategy and position itself close to its competitors so consumers can make a direct comparison when they purchase, or whether it wants to position itself away from its competitors.

Perceptual mapping is a research tool commonly used to help develop or evaluate a corporate design positioning strategy, and determine how consumers perceive a brand, product or product range. Through the use of an X-Y axis designers can arrange and plot market research data visually using comparator terms such as cost, quality and impact, and map their target market and audience.

A typical perceptual map might explore consumers' perceptions of a brandscape by evaluating products on the two dimensions of radical/conservative and expensive/affordable. What might emerge from such mapping is that several companies produce products that are perceived by consumers to be positioned close to each other. This would indicate a competitive grouping and crowded marketplace, and a company wishing to introduce a new product might then look for an area of the map free from competitors – a 'gap in the market'. Some perceptual maps provide additional data by using different-sized dots or circles to indicate the sales volume or market share of the various competing products.

As well as displaying consumers' perceptions of products, a perceptual map can also display the desires of a target consumer group. Consumers can be asked to map their ideal product, through identifying the point where the two dimensions combine to form what is described as an ideal point. By plotting the ideal points of a sample target consumer group, one can identify clusters of high demand, or demand voids. Designers developing new products will usually look for areas of high density of ideal points, and areas without many competitive

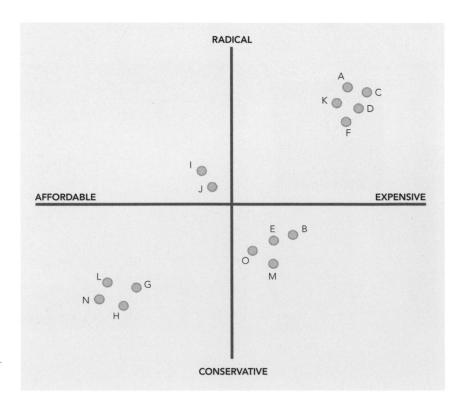

Fig. 13
This perceptual mapping diagram shows how consumers perceive rival products in terms of price (on the X axis) and innovation (on the Y axis). This can help identify overcrowded markets as well as gaps in the market.

rivals, in order to locate a fertile market opportunity. Maps are plotted on the basis of consumers' subjective perceptions, so to ensure reliable data, researchers usually collate the views of large focus groups.

Perceptual maps can help identify where a company could launch a new product, by providing qualitative information, such as how consumers perceive their rivals, alongside quantitative information, such as the average price and quality of rival products.

Personas

Personas are fictional characters that are typically based on real-life observations of archetypal users with specific objectives and needs. Personas are created to represent groups of users within a targeted demographic who might all use particular products, brands and services in a similar way. Thus, personas, sometimes referred to as 'character profiles' or 'pen portraits', are a useful method for segmenting different types of users in a crowded marketplace. A persona will typically include specific information such as a fictitious name, age, occupation, educational qualifications, employment history, hobbies, details of their family and friends, and what kinds of products and brands they regularly purchase.

Personas are particularly useful during the exploratory stages of the design process, as they allow product designers to gain a good understanding of their customers' expectations and needs in a relatively cheap and straightforward manner. They will help you to understand the people who will be using your product, service or system – and by designing for an archetypal persona you can, in turn, satisfy the broader group of consumers represented by that archetype.

When developing a set of personas you should start with a foundation document that includes references to existing data that informs your initial assumptions. You should then develop the primary personality on this skeleton, fleshing out the character by determining important characteristics such as goals, roles, behaviour, physical attributes, skills, needs, preferences, opinions and environmental context. Taking into account any cultural differences, you should choose values that are meaningful and believable to the target consumer, and ensure the personas you develop are robust enough to be used throughout the product design development process. Remember that a good persona tells a rich and meaningful story.

Once you have developed your personas you can use them to test your product designs in development. A well-constructed persona provides an invaluable visual and anecdotal profile based on in-depth research of 'real' users, and they can help you to understand how people might actually use a product. It is important to continually evaluate the cultural and contextual relevance of your qualitative personas with quantitative validation through testing; most researchers 'retire' or 're-imagine' a batch of personas after 12 months use to ensure they use on-trend archetypes informed by up-to-date demographic statistics.

The use of personas has come in for some criticism in recent years. Several design researchers have claimed that there are practical implementation issues with personas in that they can lead to a 'cloak of smug customer-centricity' and can actually increase any disconnect between the design team and real users. However, other studies of the use of personas in design projects suggest that they can improve communication between design teams and facilitate more constructive and effective user-focused discussions.

Fig. 14
Collage developed in a workshop situation to examine consumer trends.

Product collage

Product collage involves participants using image and mood boards to support their understanding and perceptions of issues. This image-based method helps participants articulate often complex and interrelated themes, and place them in an explicit context. Collaging is a generative technique, which enables existing and/or potential users to create visually rich data in response to a set of questions or assignments. The users are encouraged to discuss their thoughts and actions during the production of the collage/s, helping to provide deeper insights for the design research team.

A typical collage is a collection of images selected and assembled by the participants in response to a brief set by the researcher. The images provide more than just the visually rich description of a mood board; they also provide the opportunities for analysis and interpretation of the participants' personal narratives, and the socio-cultural interpretation of the images themselves and that of their authors/creators.

Collage enables participants to convey their thoughts and feeling in words, pictures and a combination of the two. It allows participants to articulate their personal narratives, and provides an insight into their feelings, desires and prejudices. It is argued that this technique paints a richer, more emotional picture than text-based methods, such as questionnaires.

Designers conducting research are often frustrated by the constraints of 'traditional' methods of research. For this reason collage is becoming increasingly popular. It allows designers to express their own subjective and intuitive ideas about a concept, and provides a visual outlet for expression and debate. It is an analytic method that can be used to visualize a narrative conceptually; its visual and textual interface can help both designers and consumers to generate visual images to express verbal concepts, and to formulate ways of capturing, structuring and describing the visual experiences that they may have when viewing or using a product. It can help designers 'see' visual research data in a new way, and it provides an opportunity to triangulate these findings with qualitative data from users, and statistical data generated by more traditional research methods.

Extreme users

Extreme users are individuals who are either extremely familiar or completely unfamiliar with a particular product, service or system. Whereas conventional user interviews collect information from users at the centre of an intended target market, extreme user interviews draw upon the perspectives and experiences of these users from the edges or extremities of the target market.

Extreme user interviews are an effective way of highlighting key issues surrounding particular designed products, services or systems – they can often open up unexpected areas and issues, providing insights for future design improvements or opportunities. Extreme user interviews are an extension of the 'lead user' interviews originally developed by Dr Eric von Hippel of Massachusetts Institute of Technology (MIT), and first described in a 1986 issue of the journal *Management Science*.

Generally speaking, the extreme users method involves three major steps:

1. Identification of user needs and trends
2. Identification of extreme users
3. Conduct interviews

Extreme-user interviews are based on the notion that innovative products can be designed and developed by identifying leading or extreme trends in the specific marketplace the product is being aimed at. For example, a company seeking to create an innovative product in the area of audio-video equipment may seek out advice and opinions from a variety of extreme types of users, including DJs, musicians, music fans, producers, or others who use, play, listen, write and record music and video as part of their usual day-to-day activities. The network of friends and colleagues of these extreme users could also be a rich source of information.

Lead or extreme users will likely have knowledge and insights that will be 'outside' or 'beyond' the market, and possess more extreme needs than the typical user. By asking, listening and learning from extreme users, designers will create opportunities for coming up with breakthrough ideas and truly innovative products that may not have surfaced using conventional user interview techniques.

Case Study

Héctor Serrano and Victor Vina's netObjects

Introduction
In 2004, the Spanish artists Héctor Serrano and Victor Vina developed 'netObjects' – a collection of objects for the home that presented real-time information from the internet.

Objectives
The objects included in the collection were designed for eight fictional characters, who were all extreme users of media.

Methods
The artists chose everyday objects, including a jewellery box, an umbrella and a cuckoo clock, and connected them to the internet using wireless networks. Each object was given one simple function, such as finding a partner for a date, getting a weather report or catching the news headlines. These concepts propose an alternative way to enjoy online content at home, and each one of the interactive products was based on the testimonials of extreme users. There are eight netObjects altogether:

1. netGossip keeps you abreast of all the latest gossip relating to celebrities and the rich and famous. 'What is Lady Gaga's latest fashion statement?'

2. netCuckoo delivers news headlines every 15 minutes. It has a selector for right or left wing journalism, and can be activated by pulling the switch. 'Do you want the *Daily Mail* or the *Guardian* view on the latest political scandal?'

3. netPeep broadcasts thousands of live shows of delicious, vivacious girls for your viewing pleasure. 'Do you fancy small, medium or large?'

4. For the worldwide investor, netGlobe provides real-time stock-market quotes direct to your desk. 'How is BP's latest share price?', 'Should I buy or sell my RBS stock?'

5. Take a look at netUmbrella and check out the weather forecast for your city. 'Will it rain or shine tomorrow?', 'Do I need my coat this afternoon?'

6. netFlirt prints personal contact ads just for you. For men and women seeking men or women. Or seeking that little bit more?

7. netGoal will alert you and play back goals scored by or against your team. 'How are United doing this evening?', 'Has Maxi scored again?'

8. Rub netFuture and it will read your hands. Enter your date of birth for greater accuracy. 'Will I have a long life?', 'Will I be rich?'

Results
The netObjects collection gives body to specific themes – from the latest headlines to personal contact ads, stockmarket quotes to horoscopes – and by doing so questions the role of networked appliances in the domestic environment.

Left to right, top to bottom, netObjects collection of everyday objects for the home that present real time information from the web: netGossip; netCuckoo; netPeep; netGlobe; netUmbrella; netFlirt; netGoal; netFuture.

Case Study

Seymourpowell: Axe/Lynx brand DNA

Introduction

Founded in 1984 by Richard Seymour and Dick Powell, Seymourpowell is a London-based design and innovation company that focuses on research-informed design. They aim to combine up-to-date intelligence about people, markets and businesses with forecasting and interpreting the vital implications of user behaviours to develop future scenarios. This holistic approach to design development was employed for their recent work for deodorant brand, Axe.

Objective

Axe deodorant – known as Lynx in the UK – has huge brand awareness among consumers, thanks to a long-running and impactful advertising campaign. But the challenge of keeping such a brand competitive requires constant research and development.

Axe employed Seymourpowell to analyze the brand's success, identify consumers' attitudes, and find out how the brand's attributes could be consistently delivered through product design and retail packaging. An ability to deconstruct and analyze consumer perceptions of products and services allows brand owners to manipulate the key ingredients in their ongoing design language.

Methods

Seymourpowell stripped the brand to its essentials, using detailed ethnographic and product research to reveal what the product really meant to consumers. The next challenge was to identify how the brand's existing emotional qualities – humour, sexual attraction and a play on male insecurity – could be reflected in the ongoing design of the product packaging itself. It became clear there was a duality to the Axe persona: on the one side, the confident sexual male, on the other side, an ugly/spotty/geeky male hoping to get the girl. Advertising campaigns had set up this tension, but the product itself needed to reflect the same personality, being confident and mature while delivering a feeling of fun and knowing playfulness.

Results

The result of this process was the Neutron can. Its twist cap takes cues from zoom camera lenses and similar boy-friendly gadgets, encouraging playful, tactile engagement with the product. The can received positive press coverage and scooped a silver medal at the Starpack Awards, where judges praised its 'excellent shelf impact and consumer convenience'. More importantly, Seymourpowell placed Axe/Lynx's fundamental brand attributes under the microscope and translated them into a design language that can be employed by the client again and again.

Opposite: The Axe/Lynx brand Neutron deodorant can. The twist cap takes cues from zoom camera lenses.

Case Study

MJV Tecnologia e Inovação: SMS Coach

Introduction

Chronic medical conditions such as diabetes, hypertension and cancer pose significant and complex problems for societies all over the world. Such conditions generally do not pose an immediate risk to an individual's health but, if not managed and cared for properly, can cause serious complications in the long term, often leading to the death of the patient. Chronic diseases usually involve high medical costs, and they have a major and life-long impact on a patient's quality of life.

Objective

MJV were asked by a Brazilian health insurance company to study the unmet needs of chronically ill patients. The main motivation behind this project was to identify opportunities that could lead to a reduction of costs through health monitoring, as well as an increase in the health and wellbeing of individuals.

Methods

MJV adopted a 'context research' approach, where the design team approached the context of the problem from the perspective of the company (the client) as well as the end-user (the client's customer). Two initial research methods were used for a better understanding of the context being studied – a review of the literature and an ethnographic study. The data collected was organized, and patterns and similarities identified. Personas were then used to communicate the research findings to the client.

Five personas were created for this project. The personas and brainstorming sessions were used to stimulate the generation of ideas and enable the testing of quick-and-dirty prototypes. Employees from the health insurance company participated in these activities together with MJV designers and industry experts. This generated a selection of almost 70 ideas, which formed the basis for the development of tangible solutions to be tested with chronic patients, doctors and policy-holders.

Results

Five of the near 70 ideas initially generated were developed into experience prototypes. One of these was the 'SMS Coach', a mobile phone-based service created to involve and assist (specifically diabetic and hypertensive) patients in leading healthier lifestyles by using mobile telecommunications technology.

After registering with the SMS Coach, users benefit from coaching and monitoring activities provided by a virtual stakeholder, the provider or the 'coach', facilitated through a typical mobile phone's SMS interface. Users of the service consult with service providers by messaging the phrase 'Well Being' to a predetermined mobile number. After this, users are invited to share information such as diet and exercising habits. This information is used by service providers to coach users to reach goals that will eventually lead to healthier habits.

MJV developed a number of quick-and-dirty prototypes and iteratively tested them in user trials. Initial results suggest that the SMS Coach may indeed succeed in supporting healthier chronic patients and result in fewer costs for the health insurance company.

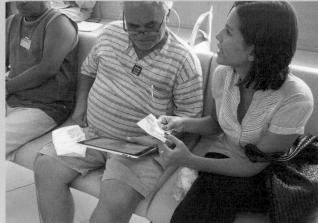

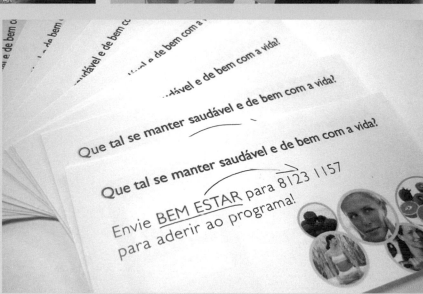

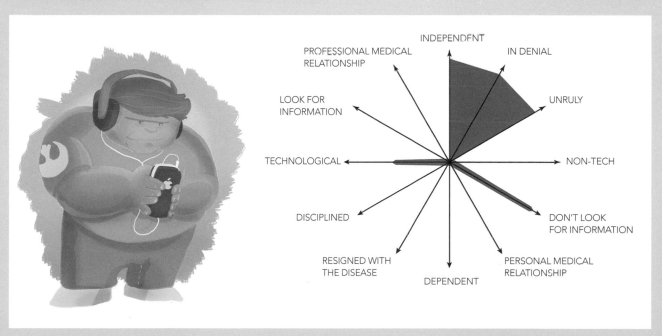

The 'SMS Coach', a mobile phone-based service created to support diabetic and hypertensive patients lead healthier lifestyles.

How to create a great questionnaire

It's important to give respondents enough time and an adequate place to complete their questionnaire.

Before setting off on writing your questionnaire you should use the following steps as a guide:

1. Decide what information you want to gather from the questionnaire.

2. Keep the questionnaire as short as possible, asking only those questions that will provide the information you need.

3. Use a casual, conversational style, making the questions easy for almost anyone to understand.

4. Structure the questionnaire so that the questions follow a logical order and evolve from general to specific.

5. Use multiple-choice questions whenever possible. This helps the respondent to better understand the purpose of your question and will reduce the time it takes to complete the questionnaire.

6. Avoid leading questions that might generate false positive responses. For example, the question 'How great was the service provided by our excellent waiters?' should be 'How was the service provided by our waiters?'.

7. Use the same rating scale throughout. For example, if the scale is from 1 to 5, with 5 being the most positive, keep that same scale for all of the questions requiring a rating.

8. Test the questionnaire on 10 to 15 people before you produce it for mass distribution. Conduct an interview with each of those respondents after he or she completes the survey to determine if your questions were easily understood and easy to answer.

Following these simple steps will help you get the most out of your questionnaire and go some way to obtaining the information you require from people.

Question sequence

In general, questions should flow logically from one to the next. To achieve the best response rates, questions should flow from the least sensitive to the most sensitive, from the factual and behavioural to the attitudinal, and from the more general to the more specific.

Basic rules for questionnaire item construction

— Use statements that are interpreted in the same way by members of different sub-populations of the population of interest.
— Use statements where people that have different opinions or traits will give different answers.
— Think of having an 'open' answer category after a list of possible answers.
— Use only one aspect of the construct you are interested in per item.
— Use positive statements and avoid negatives or double negatives.
— Do not make assumptions about the respondent.

— Use clear and comprehensible wording, easily understandable for all educational levels.
— Use correct spelling, grammar and punctuation.
— Avoid more than one question per item (e.g. 'Do you like strawberries and potatoes?').
— Write down the central idea or use a central multicoloured image that signifies the mind map subject.
— Think up new ideas related to the central idea.
— Use themes to provide the main divisions of the mind map.
— Enclose each theme with an outline that hugs the shape created by the branches.
— Make sure that the lines that support each key word are the same length as the word and 'organically' connect to the central image.
— Print so that each word used is clear and legible.
— Try to use single key words uncluttered by adjectives or definitions.
— Use colour for vividness and to enhance memory recollection.

Completed 'I want to be a Designer because...' questionnaires.

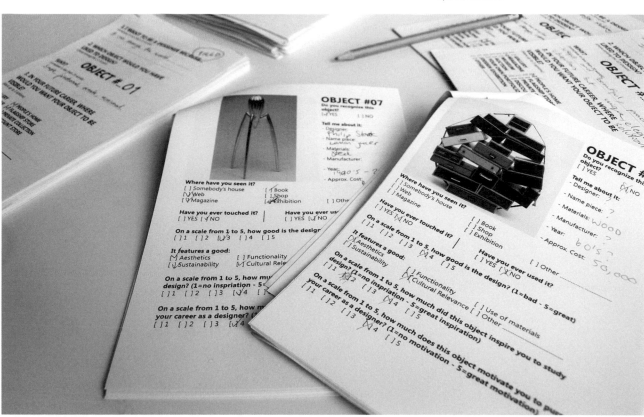

How to conduct great interviews

Interviews are a commonly used research technique, enabling design researchers to pursue in-depth information around a topic of research, and/or to follow up on the results of a questionnaire. Interviews can follow a number of formats:

Informal, conversational interview
This format doesn't use a set of predetermined questions, and adopts a flexible 'go with the flow' approach.

General interview guide approach
This format ensures that the same general areas of information are collected from each interviewee; this provides more focus than the informal approach, but still allows a degree of freedom and adaptability in getting information from subjects.

Standardized, open-ended interview
In this format the same open-ended questions are asked of all interviewees.

Closed, fixed-response interview
This highly structured format asks all interviewees the same set of questions and asks them to choose answers from among the same set of alternatives.

Video still images of 30-second face-to-face interviews conducted by Johnny Weir.

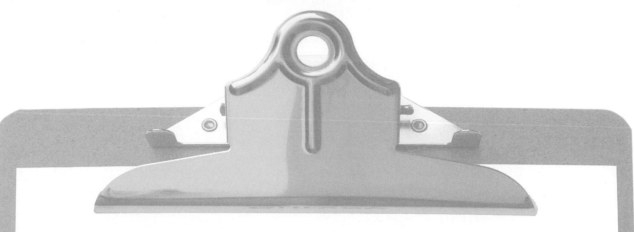

Step-by-step Guidelines

— Choose a setting with no distractions and where the interviewee will feel comfortable.

— Explain the purpose of the interview.

— Address terms of confidentiality, explaining who will get access to the respondent's answers and how their answers will be analyzed. If their comments are to be used as quotes, you must get their written permission to do so.

— Explain the format of the interview you are conducting and its nature. Indicate how long the interview usually takes.

— Tell the interviewee how to get in touch with you later if they want to.

— Ask them if they have any questions before you start with the interview.

— Ask for permission to record the interview, as you can't count on your memory to recall their answers.

— Get the respondent involved in the interview as soon as possible.

— Before asking about controversial matters (such as feelings and conclusions), first ask about facts.

— Intersperse fact-based questions throughout the interview – this will avoid long lists of fact-based questions, which tend to leave respondents disengaged.

— Ask questions about the present before questions about the past or future.

— Occasionally verify the tape or video recorder (if used) is working.

— Ask one question at a time.

— Attempt to remain as neutral as possible and don't show strong emotional reactions to the interviewee's responses.

— Encourage responses with occasional affirmations and nods of the head.

— If you take notes, be careful that this is not revealing or distracting.

— Provide a transition between major topics, for example 'We've been talking about X and now I'd like to move on to Y'.

— Don't lose control of the interview and allow the respondent to stray to another topic, take too long to answer or even begin questioning you.

— You should finish the interview by allowing the respondent to provide any other information they wish to add and their overall impressions of the interview.

— Make any additions to your written notes to clarify your findings as soon as possible after the interview to ensure you don't forget any crucial points.

— Write down any observations made during the interview that may have impacted on the process.

MAKING

Designers make models and prototypes to inform their design and decision-making processes. While these have traditionally been perceived as highly developed physical models, contemporary designers now use both terms to describe any kind of representation that is created to help designers, users and clients to understand, explore and communicate what qualities a product has, and how a user might engage with it. Thus, the terms 'models' and 'prototypes' are nowadays used to describe a range of design representations, from concept sketches through to a variety of physical, CAD and virtual models that explore and communicate design propositions and contexts.

Sketch modelling

Product design is a three-dimensional discipline, and while the immediacy of marker renderings, and the visual gloss and ease of CAD offer huge possibilities, it is essential that designers model their concepts physically and test them in the real world.

Sketch models are full-size or scale models that aim to capture the embryonic ideas emerging from the design team's initial concept development. These expressive and rapidly produced models will progress in complexity, resolution and finish until the designer or team are confident enough to progress to more time-intensive models. Sketch models are typically hand-carved or sculpted from readily available materials such as urethane foam or foam board. Due to the materials used, they are generally crude and not fully representative of the final intended design.

Sketch models enable designers to visualize their two-dimensional designs three-dimensionally. They provide an insight into sculptural aspects of a product's evolving form, and allow for quick and effective evaluation of aesthetics, ergonomics, functionality, usability, proportion, and packaging and configuration options. Designers can then develop these aspects further, as required.

Sketch models also help designers to convey their designs to others in a design team or as a final representation of a design to a client. They can be used to test public reaction to a new design, and evaluate its suitability within a market. They can also be used to test the structural integrity of a design, or to test a particular part of a design, such as a mechanism.

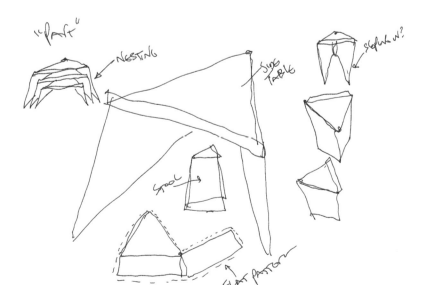

Fig. 1
Early concept sketches are quickly worked up into full-scale cardboard models by Stephen Burks during the design process for his Handmade Furniture tables. Burks believes working with full-scale models is crucial to understanding scale and usability.

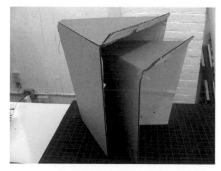

Sketch models are almost always produced to scale. This can be either smaller than actual size (i.e. 1:5, 1:10, 1:20, 1:50 or 1:100) for large items such as pieces of furniture or interiors, actual size (i.e. 1:1) or larger than actual size (i.e. 2:1 or 5:1) for very small products or for developing new mechanisms. The scale of a model also depends on the stage of development. In the early stages of a design project, when many ideas are being explored, smaller-scale models are more common.

Mock-ups

A mock-up is a life-size physical model constructed from easily fabricated materials such as rigid card, wood and foam. Such models are used to evaluate the physical interaction, scale and proportion of product design concepts. Mock-ups and simulations are most commonly used to evaluate designs during the early stages and the midway point of the design process.

Mock-ups are commonly required for bespoke furniture products, enabling designers to produce a full-size replica using inexpensive materials in order to verify a design's form, scale and ergonomics. They are often used to determine the proportions of a design and how it relates to a spatial context. Mock-ups can also be used to test the colour, finish and other specific details – factors that cannot be easily visualized or resolved through sketches or technical drawings.

Mock-ups that replicate a mechanical action or enable a physical property of a design, such as its strength, stiffness, comfort or durability, to be tested are known as test rigs. While computer modelling and analysis techniques provide designers with important insights into how a product component might perform, they are based on assumptions and approximations of actual product behaviour. Full validation of a design can only be achieved by the extensive practical testing of representative test rigs and mock-up prototypes. Such testing is usually undertaken by engineers working closely with the design team to ensure that the learning gained through the tests are fed directly into the integrated development of a product for production.

Mock-ups that do not incorporate any product styling and are only intended to demonstrate the basic mechanism of a product are typically referred to as proof of concept models. These are used to 'prove' the viability of a

Fig. 2
Simple 2D paper mock-up, created at actual size, for a new mobile phone concept.

Fig. 3
(Above) Cardboard and polystyrene models of
Edward Barber and Jay Osgerby's Pavilion Chair.
These were created at an early stage of the
development to test comfort and stability.

Fig. 4
(Left) CAD prototype of a digital scrapbook.
Digital prototypes (CAD models) are a relatively
quick and effective way of testing concepts
without having to physically make them.

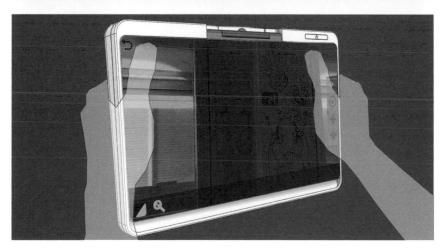

potential design approach, such as a product's range of motion, mechanics,
sensors or architecture.

Mock-ups are a key development and standards testing tool, helping
designers to validate design options and determine where further development
and testing are necessary. They also provide the engineering team with the
opportunity to do a final check for design flaws or possible last-minute
improvements. The cost of producing mock-ups is often outweighed by the
savings made by avoiding going into production with a design that needs
subsequent improvement.

The number of mock-ups required varies from project to project, and
depends on the scale and, indeed, the budget available. However, the need to

evaluate a product's form, composition, materiality and production processes can only be properly met through intensive prototyping. The development of the Dyson DC01 vacuum cleaner (p.110), for example, required thousands of prototypes before innumerable issues were resolved and the concept reached production.

Paper prototyping

Paper prototypes provide a quick way to visualize, organize and articulate basic design concepts. They are widely used in the design and development of new products. Designers can use this method to sketch out and evaluate the basic functionality and usability aspects of their concepts, and assess whether or not user interfaces meet users' expectations and needs.

Paper prototypes are meant to have a 'throwaway' quality. They are intended to be rough, hand-drawn, sketchy representations of a product's interface. Some paper prototypes can be hand-drawn, while others use printed screenshots. Although aspects of paper prototyping can appear rather simple – crude, even – this method of usability testing can result in significant insights and valuable feedback.

Paper prototyping is not a new research method. It has its origins in the mid-1980s, when companies including IBM, Microsoft and Apple started adopting the technique in the design and development of many of their products. Nowadays, paper prototyping and digital paper prototyping are widespread in the evaluation of products with a significant degree of screen-based user interaction. Paper prototypes are also often used in conjunction with eye-tracking software, which can record a user's eye movements as they perform key tasks while using a product, to evaluate and refine new computer interfaces.

Paper prototyping can be used for virtually any type of human–computer product interface, such as a web-based service or a mobile hand-held device. The main aim is to get rapid feedback from intended users while a design is in its early stages of development. Usability testing involves recruiting and selecting a suitable number of users who represent the target market(s), and having them perform realistic tasks using the prototype. A session typically includes a facilitator (someone trained in usability) to run the session, with members of the design and development team as observers, taking notes about what works well for the users and what confuses them.

In addition to usability testing, product design and development teams also find that paper protyping can be a useful way of generating design ideas and conducting internal interface reviews.

Paper prototyping has a number of advantages over other forms of prototyping:

— It is a very fast way to mock up an interface.
— It can detect a wide variety of problems in an interface, including many serious issues.
— It allows an interface to be refined based on user feedback before any real physical implementation begins.
— It facilitates a multidisciplinary approach.
— It encourages creativity from the design and development team as well as the end-users.

Fig. 5
Development models for a new range of ceramic ware, including concept sketches, paper prototypes and clay models.

Fig. 6
The creation of quick-and-dirty prototypes is an enormously valuable tool for helping designers during the iterative design and evaluation cycles. Shown above and below right are various quick-and-dirty prototypes for a new mobile phone concept.

Quick-and-dirty prototypes

Quick-and-dirty prototypes are used as a quick way to communicate a concept design idea to other members of the product design team. From this the team can then evaluate, reflect and refine its ideas before progressing further. The prototypes are built quickly and with any materials that may be to hand – the focus here is on speed rather than quality. Many design projects have short timescales with very demanding deadlines; quick-and-dirty prototypes can help designers 'cut corners' in order to save both time and other valuable resources.

The 'rough and ready' nature of quick-and-dirty prototypes encourages exploration too – design teams will more readily add, remove or change elements of a design that they have invested less time in and that has less emotional significance than a more 'polished' prototype. The process is cheap, quick and open to interpretation. It also enables designers to focus on the essence of a concept, and avoid getting bogged down trying to resolve details.

Quick-and-dirty prototypes provide 'good enough' or approximate results rapidly. Generally speaking, these prototypes will be used in conjunction with established evaluation methods such as focus groups, interviews or field observations, but applied in a less formal way than is usual. For instance, in order to save time the design team may cut some corners in the selection and recruitment of participants, reduce the number of users providing feedback and/or reduce the scope of the product proposal's evaluation.

Product concepts evolve through a number of iterative design and evaluation cycles. That is, designers create prototypes and evaluate their strengths and weaknesses, often by assessing verbal or written descriptions of the proposed product design against users' requirements to evaluate their suitability or otherwise. Quick-and-dirty prototypes are an enormously valuable tool for designers during this process. Generally speaking, they will be constructed using a range of inexpensive materials such as paper, card, glue, sticky tape, wood and polystyrene foam, although it is increasingly common these days for many product proposals to be simulated via screen-based interactive prototypes using off-the-shelf computer software, with companies offering specialist product design services in computer visualization and modelling.

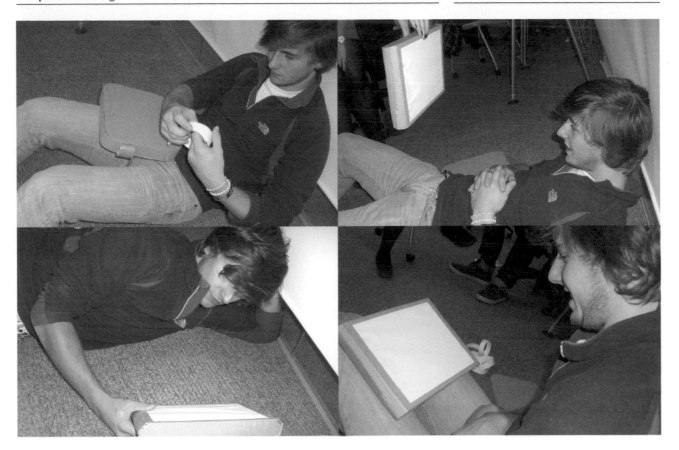

Experience prototyping

While prototypes have traditionally been perceived as highly developed physical models, contemporary designers now use the term to describe any kind of representation that is created to help designers, users and clients to understand, explore and communicate what qualities a product has, and how a user might engage with it.

A recent development has been the widespread use of prototypes that focus on the experiential aspects of a design. Experience prototyping, as it is known, is a useful research tool for detecting unanticipated problems or opportunities as well as evaluating ideas.

The discipline of product design has been transformed by the move from a manufacturing economy to that of an experience economy, with experience itself becoming the product. Consumers no longer merely consume products but lifestyles, with products not merely functional objects but who we imagine ourselves to be. Experience prototypes are a vital device for addressing these design challenges – they demonstrate what it is like to actually use a product in a given situation, and provide findings that can help develop a product's experiential qualities through an iterative prototyping process.

Experience prototypes, often fully working and robust enough for trialing with end-users over periods of time, can play a vital role throughout the design process and not just at the concept stage. They enable the design team, users and clients alike to engage with a concept and help prompt vital dialogue between all the stakeholders. They help to ensure a streamlined development process that avoids costly mistakes or delays in bringing a product to market.

Having a working interactive model (experience prototype) enables the design team to learn from a simulation of the proposed product's use in a variety of different contexts and gain valuable insights into what the experience might be like for users. This can help them to uncover any unanticipated issues and needs, and assess the utility and other aspects of the product proposal.

Fig. 7
Quick-and-dirty development prototypes exploring the concept of computing on the go.

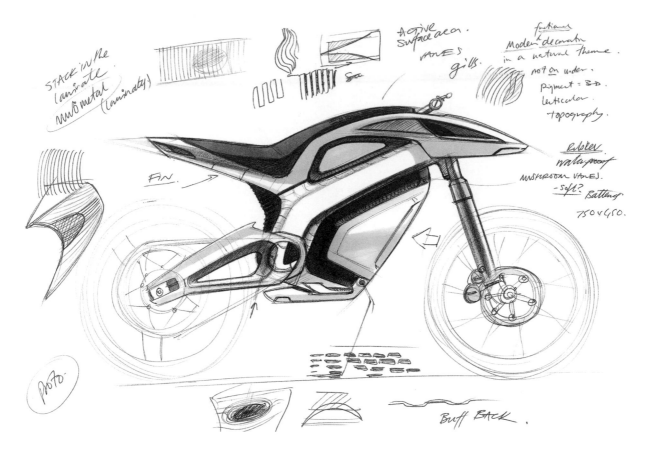

Fig. 8
Development sketch for the ENV motorcycle by Seymourpowell with Intelligent Energy.

Appearance models

An appearance model closely simulates the look of a production product. It is used to communicate a design to clients and users. An appearance model typically does not function the way a production product would, if it has any functionality at all. Normally internal components do not exist, while all moving parts are fixed in their most preferred or typical position. Sometimes the product is constructed from particular materials so that its weight is represented accurately. This helps assess how a proposed product (e.g. a laptop computer) will fit into its environments of use as well as determining whether its physical characteristics are appropriate for the product's purpose.

While large-scale products such as cars, bikes and boats are often presented as a 1:4 or 1:10 scale models, most consumer product appearance models are life-size/actual-size. The primary purpose of such a model is to evaluate a design's aesthetics and ergonomics, and convey detailed finishes, textures and colours. It allows designers to explore the basic size, look and feel of a product.

Appearance models are often hand-carved, sculpted or machined from a solid block of inexpensive material such as foam, plastic, wood or clay, and subsequently finished and painted to look like the desired end product. Due to the materials used, these models are not especially durable and should be handled with care. Appearance models are used for market research, exhibition display, executive review and approval, and product literature photographs. Due to their delicate nature they are not commonly used for interaction and handling by representative users or consumers.

In the past, appearance prototypes were commonly made out of clay; they are subsequently still referred to as clay models in some design agencies and companies. Car companies still do use 'clay' – a form of industrial plasticine – for

Fig. 9
Full-scale appearance models created as
physical prototypes, in clay, to give an idea of
vehicle mass and rider ergonomics, and as a
CAD model, which demonstrates the soft
curves of the bodywork.

sketch and appearance models, as it is a malleable material that can be easily sculpted, when determining a product's form, proportions and surface tension. Its continued use helps retain the strong practical, aesthetic and conceptual connections between sculpture and design.

Empathy tools

Over the last decade the design industry and society as a whole has begun to treat older people and the disabled differently, moving away from the outdated perspective of viewing them as special cases, and embracing a new social-equality agenda that aims to integrate them into the mainstream of everyday life through a more inclusive approach to the design of products. These welcome changes have been reinforced with the passing of equality and discrimination legislation, which designers are legally obliged to adhere to. By addressing the needs of these users, designers can produce better designs that improve how a broad range of users experience their product designs, increase their potential customer base, and ensure a more equal and cohesive society. Designers need to be aware that inclusive design is an integrated approach to design that extends to all stages of the design process; it is not simply a stage that can be bolted on.

By empathizing with users, designers are better able to embed inclusive design within the design process and, as result, produce mainstream products that are pleasurable, desirable and satisfying to use. Many companies and designers, while agreeing with the basic principles of designing inclusively, pay lip service to the practice. They assume that if a product is deemed easy to use then they are adequately covering their social responsibilities, or naively assume that it is always possible – or indeed appropriate – to design a product to address the needs of an entire population.

To avoid such pitfalls and promote an inclusive design agenda, designers need to develop an awareness of the needs of users with different capabilities through empathy and learn how to accommodate them into the design cycle. This design approach, based on the observations of real-user actions and behaviour, is exemplified by the design approach of IDEO, and their use of empathy tools. Empathy tools, also known as 'capability simulators' are a commonly used inclusive-design research method. These are physical or software devices that designers can use to reduce their ability to interact with a product, and therefore gain a sense of the experience had by users with disabilities or special conditions.

Fig. 10
Tom Bieling of Design Research Lab, Berlin, conducting self-experience research into the way blind and partially sighted people interact with an exhibit.

Weighted gloves or sports braces, for example, can be worn to reproduce a loss of dexterity or movement, or spectacles can be smeared with grease to simulate a loss of vision.

Such quick and cheap devices help designers to experience the abilities of different users, seeing the world through their eyes and gaining a deeper understanding of their issues, needs and desires. These tools can be used throughout the design process to help simulate the physical and cognitive issues that a design needs to address. However, no capability simulation device can ever truly reproduce what it is like to live with a particular capability reduction on an everyday basis, and as such they should never be considered as a replacement for involving real users in developing, designing and evaluating a product.

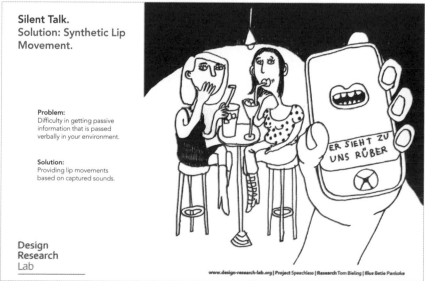

Fig. 11
Product concepts generated by Bieling's research, with a group of hearing-impaired people, into problems surrounding deaf communications. He believes that such products should not only address the needs of a niche group but also widen the field for potential use by a larger group of people in different contexts.

Fig. 12
A bodystorming session where the researchers are physically experiencing and testing a new spatial design layout.

Bodystorming

Bodystorming is a useful method that supports empathic working, idea generation and prototyping. It involves physically experiencing a situation in order to derive new ideas, and is especially useful when trying to resolve social and spatial design problems.

In this technique the design team imagines what it would be like if a concept existed and then sets up a scenario and acts out roles, with or without appropriate props, focusing on the intuitive responses prompted by such physical enactment. This technique has been criticized by some design researchers due to the fact that it is often carried out by designers rather than the potential users of the final product, and as such is not a genuine user-centred approach.

Bodystorming helps design teams to generate and quickly test a range of context and behaviour-driven concepts, such as eating on an aeroplane, selecting a radio station in a car or ordering a meal in a drive-through restaurant. It has also been successfully used to shed light on design projects such as airline passenger seat design and layout. The goal of the technique is to prompt new ideas – perhaps some that are unexpected – via the physical experience of a situation. A bodystorming session can take anything from ten minutes to one hour, depending on the complexity of the situation and the roles being played out. It can involve one or two individuals, or small or large groups of participants.

Bodystorming can help to generate ideas that might not be realizable by conventional methods such as sketching or model making. It helps create empathy in the context of possible solutions for prototyping. If you get fixated in your idea generation phase, bodystorming can help get you thinking about alternative ideas. It can also be extremely useful in the context of prototyping spatial design concepts, as it focuses on the physical sensations surrounding a design problem.

Bodystorming is a relatively simple method to employ. The aim is to physically 'act out' the design proposition. First, create a list of tasks that you wish to test during the session. Next, go through the list of tasks one at a time. As you are working through each task, verbalize what you are experiencing (e.g. challenges, surprises, other interesting observations). At the same time, ask the other members of the design team to make observations and take notes of what they see and hear.

At the end of the session the design team should answer the following questions:

1. What did you learn from the bodystorming exercise?
2. What surprised you about going through the bodystorming exercise?
3. What did you learn from doing the bodystorming exercise that you couldn't have learned any other way?
4. How can you imagine applying this bodystorming exercise to other design challenges?

Rapid prototyping

Rapid prototyping is the automatic construction of detailed physical objects from computer data using a range of 3D printing technologies. It first became available during the 1980s. Initially the process could only manufacture prototypes that could serve as a basis for discussion, as they didn't possess the required levels of detail required for serious product evaluation and testing. Today, the range of rapid prototyping technologies has developed enormously and this method can now be used for all stages of the design process, from concepts and appearance models, through to functional prototypes and mock-ups.

Rapid prototyping technologies are also increasingly being used to manufacture production-quality parts in relatively small numbers, and a number of designers, such as Patrick Jouin and Marcel Wanders, have begun to produce one-off and batch-produced products using the technique's unique 'growing' qualities as a viable manufacturing process.

Rapid prototyping is often used to check the design of parts before committing to production tooling. It enables designers to develop a functional prototype model in either short or medium production runs to support a client's development programme. This is necessary when specific functional details and material properties are integral to the finished part design. A range of different materials and 3D printing techniques can be used, and subsequently finished by plating, resin reinforcing and painting. Stereolithography, which creates models in plastic, is arguably the most commonly used process, while other techniques produce models in paper or metal. Designers produce detailed designs on screen, and then output this technical data for production through a form of 3D printing, similar in concept to inkjet printing. Instead of building up text, rapid prototyping actually constructs a 3D object, starting from a computer file by adding one slice on top of another using semi-liquid or powdered material.

Rapid prototyping has become an essential research and development tool in contemporary product design. It enables the quick and accurate creation of tangible physical models in order to verify design details, assembly, aesthetics and ergonomics. The various processes available allow for the layer-by-layer construction of complex models that would be difficult and time-consuming to produce using other fabrication processes, reducing manufacturing time for parts – even the most complex ones – from days, weeks or months to hours.

Fig. 13
Andreia Chaves' rapid prototype shoes. To develop the external 3D structures, Chaves collaborated with the Dutch based design studio Freedom Of Creation, and combined leather-making techniques with advanced 3D printing technology.

Fig. 14
Design Partners' G-930 Wireless Gaming Headset
for Logitech. The CAD models were used to create
physical foam models on Design Partners'
in-house four and five axis CNC (computer
numerical control) machines.

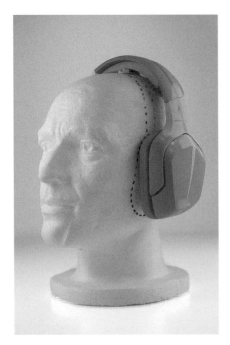

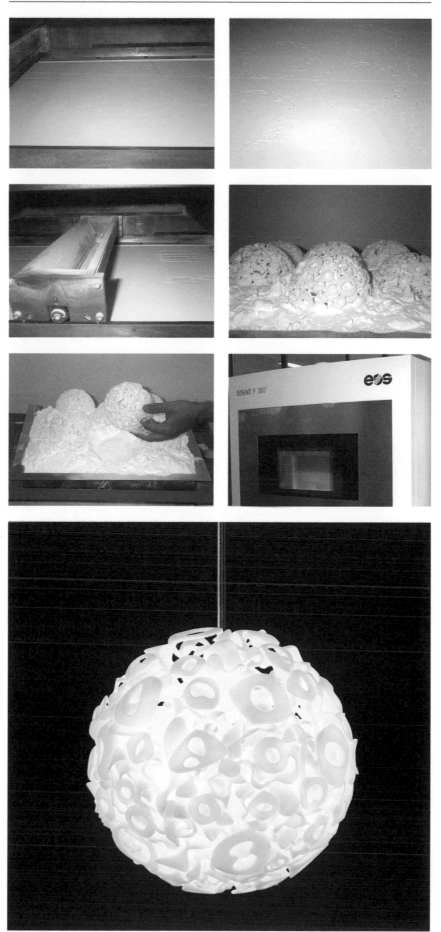

Fig. 15
The Entropia Light by Lionel T. Dean was designed to suit the process of rapid prototyping. Dean set up FutureFactories in 2002 to research the creation of products using 3D printing. The lamp was created in collaboration with Italian lighting design company Kundalini using Selective Laser Sintering, and was 'printed' using the protyping machine as a production tool.

Case Study

Dyson vacuum cleaners

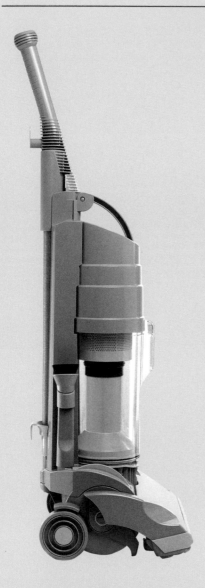

The Dyson DC01 vacuum cleaner featuring Cyclone™ technology.

Introduction

In 1978, designer and manufacturer James Dyson noticed how the air filter in his spray-finishing room was constantly clogging with powder particles (just like a vacuum cleaner bag clogs with dust). So he designed and built an industrial cyclone tower, which removed the powder particles by exerting centrifugal forces 100,000 times greater than gravity.

Objective

Having produced this innovative solution, Dyson began to consider other applications for it. He settled on exploring whether the same principle might work in a vacuum cleaner.

Methods

Five years and 5,127 iterative models later – quick-and-dirty prototypes, mock-ups, sketch and appearance models – the world's first bag-less vacuum cleaner arrived. Uninterested in new technology and wedded to vacuum bags (worth £250 million every year), major manufacturers turned Dyson and his invention away. Dyson eventually licensed his design in Japan, the home of high-tech. The Japanese loved the pink G-Force and, in 1993, the royalties allowed Dyson to manufacture a machine under his own name, the DCO1.

Results

An inventor pays substantial fees to renew patents every year. Though Dyson brushed with bankruptcy during the development years, it was money well spent. In 1999, after a lengthy court battle, Hoover was found guilty of infringing Dyson's patent. Other manufacturers, unable or unwilling to develop their own vacuum cleaners, still try to copy Dyson technology, to no avail.

James Dyson and his engineers continue to improve existing Dyson technology through extensive user trials and materials testing. Their machines now have smaller multiple cyclones, which create greater centrifugal forces, capturing more microscopic dust. After observing that the wheels on a normal upright vacuum cleaner run on a fixed axle and so can only move in straight lines, Dyson decided to address this problem too.

The resulting design, developed through numerous models and prototypes, was a vacuum cleaner that rides on a single large ball, pivoting on a single point, and allowing it to go in any direction. The Dyson Ball successfully eliminates the struggle of manoeuvering a vacuum around furniture and other obstacles, allowing the user to control the movement – not the other way around.

CAD exploded view of Dyson Ball™ technology,
and the Dyson Ball cylinder vacuum that utilizes
the technology.

Case Study

OXO Good Grips kitchen utensils

A selection of OXO Good Grips kitchen utensils including a vegetable peeler, a garlic press, a can opener, and a vegetable masher.

Introduction

In 1990 Oxo International introduced its Good Grips kitchen utensils for people whose capabilities were limited by arthritis.

Objective

Oxo's design philosophy is to make products that are easy to use for the widest possible spectrum of users.

Methods

The company moved beyond merely functional agendas and the traditional assistive model of designing for a specific disability, by focusing on meeting actual users' needs and experiences through the extensive use of empathy tools. In conjunction with New York-based Smart Design, they also created a distinct, stylish aesthetic and desirability that enabled these ergonomically designed products to cross over to a mainstream consumer audience, bringing the benefits of ergonomic inclusive design to all.

Oxo's design research approach is to ask, observe and participate. Involving large numbers of consumers in user trials and product usability testing – designing with rather than for users – undoubtedly improves the accuracy of their research and increases the possibility of uncovering unperceived issues.

Results

The financial benefits of this approach have been significant – Oxo has grown at an annual rate of over 30 per cent since the introduction of the Good Grips range, and a number of major companies have since adopted similar design strategies.

Oxo were among the first brands to realize that members of a typical design team are often not representative users, and as such it is important to involve an appropriate mix of people to input into the design process to ensure the creation of a genuinely inclusive design. All too often, commercial or time pressures mean that inclusive design and ergonomics principles are compromised or not given adequate priority until too late in the design process. The Good Grips range demonstrates that these principles can be applied at the earliest stages of the design process, defining user needs and identifying opportunities for genuine product design innovation and usability.

Case Study

Pili Wu
plastic ceramics

Introduction

Developed during the Chinese Song Dynasty, eggshell porcelain or bodiless chinaware is a unique technique which produces remarkably thin and light porcelain wares, which feel almost as thin as eggshell. These porcelain pieces can easily be seen through when held up to the light.

Objective

The fine eggshell porcelain wares are often exclusive products made in limited quantities, since the production processes are very complicated and time-consuming. The HAN Gallery set Pili Wu a brief that asked him to research these complicated processes in order to make a series of fine eggshell porcelain wares that would be much more affordable for mass markets.

Methods

Pili Wu initially conducted a series of web searches and literature reviews into the history of the manufacture of eggshell porcelain. He discovered that, traditionally, eggshell porcelains are first fired at around 800 degrees Celsius, and then treated by very experienced craftsmen to carve out excess surface material to achieve the desired thickness. In the end, the eggshell porcelain pieces are fired again at 1280 degrees to bring about the final products. However, the porcelain wares easily deform and break during the firing processes, due to the insufficient structural force rendered by the extra thin walls. Therefore, decisions had to be made to increase the strength of the porcelain ware walls, while maintaining the eggshell-like thinness. To continue the project, Pili Wu further researched using a combination of methods

including literature reviews, web searches and product analysis of existing disposable plastic wares that are commonly used in Taiwanese roadside restaurants. He found that the thin and fragile surfaces could be strengthened by a rib-like structure. The creative link was made by adapting this structure into the designs of the new set of porcelain wares.

Results

After a series of trial and error methods that included porcelain mock-ups, material testing coupled with the designer's intuition, the project has been deemed a huge success. The final mass-produced tableware family includes a fruit bowl, a candleholder, a Chinese bowl, a teapot and a set of three cups. Based on the ancient techniques, the design of Plastic Ceramics not only brings the traditional craft of eggshell porcelain wares but also the elegant lifestyle of the Chinese literati into the contemporary world. The industrial motif stamped on the base of each piece reinterprets the intricate patterns of rare antiques, giving a fresh look to the refined, lightweight porcelain tableware which are now suitable for both Chinese and Western tea-serving rituals and global table landscapes.

The Pili Wu mass-produced plastic ceramics tableware family includes a fruit bowl, a candleholder, a Chinese bowl, a teapot and a set of three cups, based on ancient techniques developed during the Chinese Song Dynasty. The design of Plastic Ceramics not only brings the traditional craft of eggshell porcelain wares but also the elegant lifestyle of the Chinese literati into the contemporary world.

Tutorial

How to conduct experience prototyping

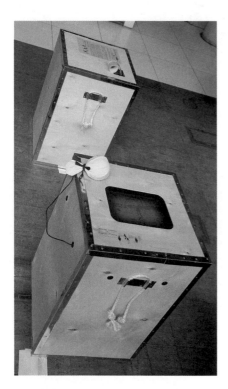

'Sensory Threads', a multi-partner collaboration led by Proboscis, is a project where groups of people can create a collective soundscape of their interactions by carrying wearable sensors. The data is fed to the 'Rumbler' where it can be experienced remotely as vibration, sound and image. The Rumbler allows people to play back the sonic and sensory explorations.

Experience prototyping allows designers, clients or users to experience a proposed product, service or system for themselves rather than witnessing a demonstration of someone else's experience. Experience is, by its very nature, highly subjective; the best way to understand the experiential qualities of using a product, service or system is to actually experience it first-hand. So, just like the rapid prototyping of physical objects or software interfaces, designers can create experience prototypes that enable users to experience a new product, service or system before it actually exists. Experience prototyping is an extremely powerful tool in gaining user insights early in the design and development process.

When creating an experience prototype you should utilize a combination of prototyping methods and materials (e.g. print and paper prototypes, bodystorming, SMS, phone calls and so on). The emphasis should be on speed – prototyping quickly, testing with users, learning, improvising and iterating. It is also vital that all user 'touchpoints' (i.e. the designed elements associated with the proposed product, including interactive internet features, printed documents, physical devices, retail outlets and call centres that the user might come into contact with) are represented as well as possible so that participants can feel immersed in the experience of the proposed product, service or system. Therefore, a rigorous 'end-to-end' experience prototype for a new bike-hire service, for example, may well include paper prototypes, screen-based interactive simulations (perhaps with mock-up hardware), SMS service, voicemail service and in-store mock-up environments that enable users to experience the complete service.

User insights gained from experience prototyping sessions can be extremely revealing and inform product, service or system propositions and other design decisions. The results of a well-executed end-to-end session might include:

— Qualitative feedback about the users' experiences.
— Reliable quantitative user interaction timings.
— Insights as to the best sequences of information presentation.
— Assessment of user comprehension.
— Identification of user errors and any underlying reasons for them.
— Identification of opportunities to improve the design.

'Sensory Threads' uses music and vibration to alert our consciousness to barely perceptible changes in the environment. Variations in the soundscape reflect changes in the wearers' interactions with each other and with the environment around them.

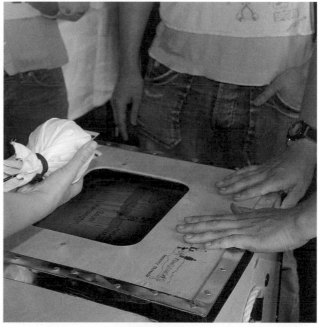

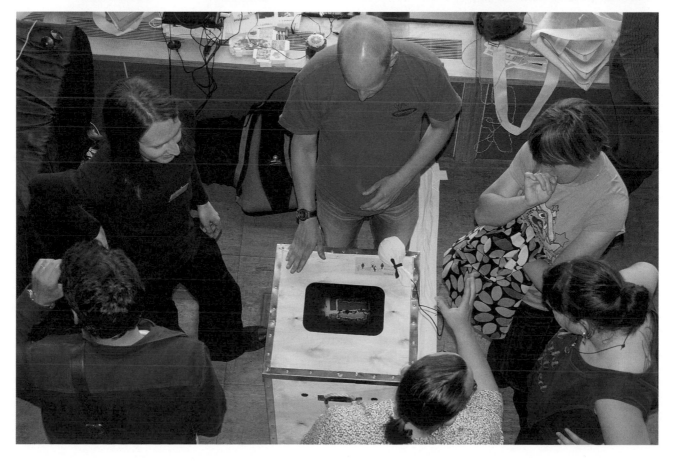

Tutorial

How to do quick-and -dirty prototyping

Quick-and-dirty prototypes are usually constructed using inexpensive materials such as paper, card, glue, sticky tape, and polystyrene foam.

Designers need results rapidly, and as a result quick-and-dirty prototyping has become an increasingly popular approach to design development. Quick-and-dirty prototypes should make your thinking tangible, giving shape to your ideas. They provide invaluable insights into how a product concept will be used, and because of their 'rough and ready' quality, people are not afraid to criticize these test models.

When considering making a quick-and-dirty prototype, you should start by determining which aspect of the user experience you want to test, and choose an appropriate 'good enough' representation to test it. This will vary according to the stage of development your project is at. For example, you might test the initial concepts behind a new chair design by building a series of skeletal structures that help define the ergonomic layout and structural requirements that need to be met. You might then build 'work-like' models that test mechanisms, and separate 'look-like' models that focus on aesthetics. By doing this in teams, you can foster a collective understanding of what you are trying to achieve, and produce a far larger number of models than would be possible working independently. You should use whatever materials are readily available – remember that this form of prototyping only needs to be good enough to test the issue at hand. Any additional refinement can actually be detrimental to the rapid iteration of design concepts. Typically you should have paper, card, foam board and hot glue at hand, but you might need to access a DIY store, depending on the nature of your designs.

As mentioned earlier, quick-and-dirty models are produced on an appropriate scale – smaller than actual size for large products, actual size for products such as mobile phones or hand-held devices, or larger than actual size for very small products. The scale you select will also depend on the stage of the design development, the time you have and the needs of the client and other stakeholders. In the early stages of a design project, for example, many smaller scale models might be more appropriate.

A quick-and-dirty prototype will necessarily cut corners. The fine details of the design proposition are not needed – the emphasis is on getting approximate and quick results and/or feedback. The quick-and-dirty method of model making is a particularly effective tool in rapidly communicating design ideas to diverse groups of stakeholders. You should also involve potential users in the design, build and evaluation of your prototypes.

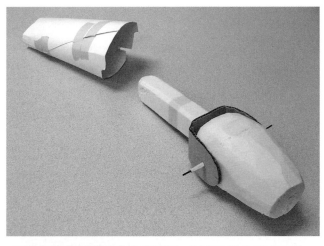

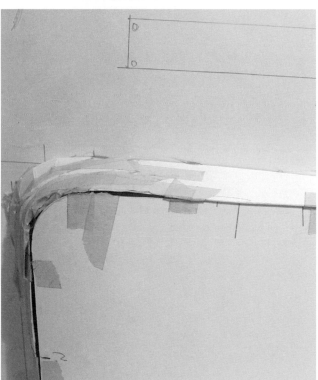

Shown here are prototypes for a folding hair dryer, using foam and paper, and a laptop bag, using cardboard with pencilled details.

TESTING

Extensive testing is a vital stage in developing and resolving a product. Designers need to test their research concepts and prototypes with end-users over periods of time to enable the design team, users and clients alike to engage with a concept and prompt vital dialogue between all the stakeholders. Testing facilitates informed decision-making, and helps ensure a streamlined development process that avoids costly mistakes or delays in bringing a product to market. This chapter introduces a variety of techniques for testing your designs, including user trials, building test rigs, and safety testing.

Scenario testing

Scenarios can help product designers communicate and evaluate design proposals within their intended context. By devising a scenario carefully with characters, narrative and context, designers can evaluate whether their design ideas will work with their intended users.

Scenario testing involves the creation of future scenarios using media such as storyboards, texts, photography, film and plays to present a product, service or concept, and then asking users to provide evaluative feedback on them. The more appropriate and convincing the presentation format, narrative and scenario, the more likely it is that the feedback will provide useful insights into a product's functional, aesthetic and behavioural qualities.

Designers require a test arena for developing and evaluating socio-cultural trends and narratives to help identify emerging values and needs. Scenarios are sketch stories that provide designers with a clear context and set of criteria they can use to design solutions for future problems. They connect research to appropriate design solutions. Scenarios are based on in-depth research findings, from ethnographic studies and interviews with stakeholders to analysis and forecasts from subject experts. These research findings then provide the basis for imaginary scenario characters. Because most products have a variety of different users, each with their own personal, professional and social concerns, you should typically create at least three different scenarios constructed around different characters in order to cover the scope of product interactions.

A set of scenarios tells you why your users need your design, what the users need the design to do, and how they need your design to do it. Scenarios aim to tell designers about how users will behave in the future, and use as yet uncreated designs and services. They promote a holistic approach to design, and help prevent designers from making design decisions based on their personal experience or preconceptions.

New products create new behaviours, and the use of scenarios can enable a design team to test new product concepts within a carefully constructed 'future context', exploring and evaluating the experiential opportunities and shifting behaviours. Scenarios are especially useful during the early stages of a product's development, when the design team can communicate, test and evaluate the validity of an early concept design to for a client and the appropriate stakeholders.

Fig. 1
Manufacturers extensively test their products through user trials and expert test drivers to ensure the required physical, tactile and dynamic qualities are met.

Fig. 2
(Opposite) Testing 'Intimate Mobiles' by Fabien Hemmert at Design Research Lab in association with Deutsche Telekom Laboratories. These experience prototypes allow for near-body telepresence in mobile telecommunication, expressing airflow, moisture and tightness. All means are explored through mobile phone-shaped and -sized boxes, which are equipped with the necessary actuators.

User trials

User trials are an effective experimental method, where a group of users test versions of products under controlled conditions. They are often carried out as part of initial research to evaluate existing products, or when a complete product is to be evaluated. Rough-and-ready prototypes may also be used, but they must be robust enough to ensure they don't degrade over the testing process and provide flawed data. User trials are often used before a design has been signed off for manufacture, and are commonly used on pre-production prototypes. They are often used as a cost-effective way of evaluating products compared to more extensive field trials, which commonly take place when a more complete product is to be tested and evaluated prior to launching into the marketplace. These studies help to inform design researchers' understanding of the specific components and actions of the user during a set task.

Setting up an effective user trial is primarily about creating an environment that enables the interaction between a product and a user to be systematically examined and measured. A representative sample of 'real' users are recruited and provided with a series of tasks to undertake within a set timetable. Information relating to the time spent completing a task or the number and types of usage errors made, is employed to compare different versions of the same product and/or user interface.

User trials commonly use video recording to capture observations, and may also rely on a team of trained observers in a controlled 'laboratory' setting to identify and record specific issues that users encounter when undertaking the tasks. Some researchers feel, though, that this level of laboratory-type observation can colour the findings – that the presence of an observer can affect the behaviour of a user – and they may choose to avoid this in order to encourage a more 'natural' interaction with the product under test by removing the possibility of users' actions and behaviour being affected by observers being present. In addition, when selecting participants the design researcher should ascertain if they have prior knowledge or experience of using a similar product.

Once the users have completed the trial they are interviewed about any difficulties they encountered or observed during the tasks. These interviews, together with a detailed analysis of the tasks captured on film, provide invaluable objective and subjective insights that can enable designers to improve the ease of use, functionality and intuitiveness of the product being developed. Videos also provide an ideal vehicle for communicating issues to the wider product development team, client and stakeholders.

While user trials are a commonly used research technique they are not without their faults. It should be noted that the research findings provided by user trials are heavily reliant on how well the users have understood the purpose and procedure of the user trial and their ability to communicate their feedback to the evaluator/s. It can also be difficult to source the required types of representative participants for user trial, and once a design researcher has assembled a user trial group, they must ensure that they don't become overly reliant on this group of individuals. Unless observation of the effects of cumulative learning is a specific aim of the research, the user groups should be changed periodically to avoid over- familiarity with the product and the testing process.

Product usability

Product usability testing is a technique used to evaluate a product – by testing it on its intended user group, which usually focuses on measuring the product's ease of use and its capacity to meet its designed purpose. Usability testing typically measures the ease of use of a specific product such as consumer products, websites, computer interfaces, and devices. Usability testing is a vital part of the design development process, enabling designers to verify whether a product is achieving its human interaction objectives and goals.

Product usability testing involves representative users being asked to test the product in a realistic environment. By observing the user's behaviour, emotions, and difficulties designers are able to identify attributes and qualities that require improvement. This type of testing also provides designers with the opportunity to see if users interact with a product in any unanticipated forms, which could, if harnessed, help contribute to the improvement of the design.

Expert reviewers are often asked to undertake initial usability testing and the benchmarking of design concepts against previous products or competitor products, as their in-depth understanding of a product type or activity can enable them to identify major usability issues early in the design process. Designers can then avoid pursuing any costly dead ends being pursued. Usability testing is especially useful at evaluating initial design concepts, as ; designers may test different elements and/or product interactions of a concept, making several small models of each component of the product/system.

Usability prototypes used in industry range from rough and ready prototypes and mock-ups to paper models, visualizations and storyboards. Using relatively inexpensive prototypes on small user groups allows designers to identify key issues early on in the design process, and minimize costly development time wasted on flawed usability approaches.

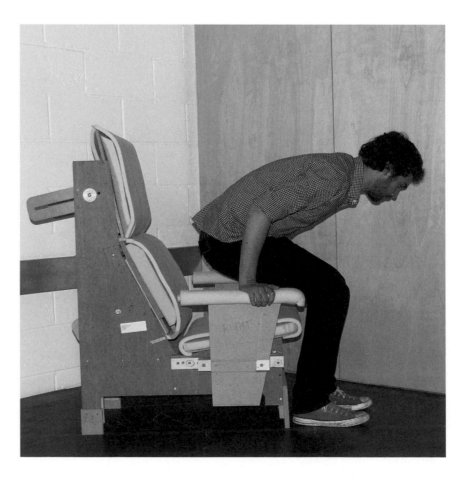

Fig. 3
Testing the ergonomics of an early MDF and cardboard rig of PearsonLloyd's hospital chair.

Metric analysis

While conducting product usability tests, designers must determine and then use a set of metrics to identify what it is they are going to measure. These metrics are often variable, and change in conjunction with the scope and goals of the design project. Qualitative design issues such as user satisfaction are often tested alongside more functional usability tasks. These metrics are then measured, producing data such as the percentage of users that completed a task, how long it took the sample group to complete the tasks, the ratio of success to failure to complete them, and the number of times users appeared frustrated. The ultimate goal of analyzing these metrics is to find/create a prototype design that users use – and like – to successfully perform given tasks and interactions.

Rapid iterative testing

Rapid iterative testing and evaluation (RITE) is a form of product usability testing that encourages testers to 'think aloud', enabling the design team observing participants to step in and change the user interface of a product, interface or service once a problem has been identified and a rapid solution been devised. The RITE technique is arguably less methodologically robust than traditional testing, but it does dramatically reduce development time, and is commonly used in the software development field.

Fig. 4
The testing of products, such as this Berghaus Tent, in extreme conditions ensures that a product is fit for purpose.

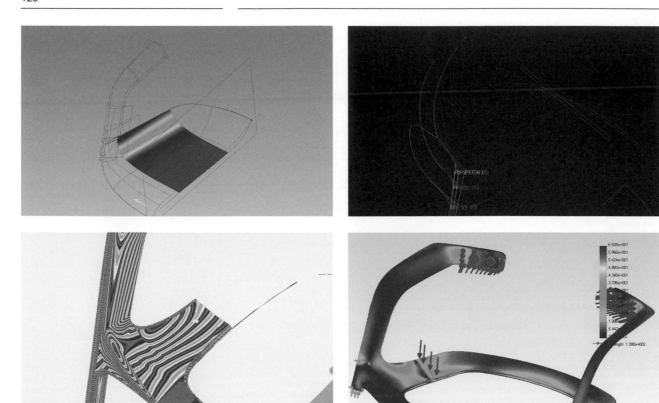

Fig. 5
Graphic CAD images demonstrating how a chair will perform under loading; from top left in a clockwise direction, they show the surface analysis of various components; the pressure each curve exerts on the model; an FEA (finite element analysis) stress analysis to understand impact on sections of the chair; an analysis of the surface using zebra curves.

Material testing

When designing a product you need to know if it will cope with every anticipated use in every expected environment. You need to know what materials it should be constructed from, whether it can be manufactured efficiently, and whether it will function at all extremes of tolerances. Selecting the right materials will be one of the most important product development decisions you will make. Failures due to poor material selection are all too common in some areas of product design, and when the wrong choice of material is made, the unanticipated costs in terms of project delays, warranty claims or product recalls, can be significant.

Failures due to poor material selection are all too common in some areas of product design. For example, in the plastics industry, it is vital that you do understand the properties of plastic, to research the material you are working with, and undertake some application-relevant testing. The sort of questions you will be seeking to answer when you are considering which material to use are: does this material have temperature- and/or time-dependant properties? Will it age physically? Will it be susceptible to chemical or environmental attack? Will it be susceptible to weathering? Will the construction result in stress problems from moulding, welding or filling? Don't rely on your experience alone or on the word of a supplier – ensure you test your designs fully.

These technical evaluations are undertaken through the use of test rigs, usually constructed in performance-testing laboratories. A test rig is the term commonly used to commonly describe a full-size or scale model that replicates a mechanical action or enables a design's physical properties (such as its strength, stiffness, comfort or durability) to be tested. While computer modelling and analysis techniques provide very important insights into the likely performance of a product and its constituent components, even the best of them are based on assumptions and approximations of actual product behaviour. The extensive practical testing and evaluation of prototypes through the use of test rigs is the only real way to validate a physical design.

An example of this is Drop Testing. This is the term used to describe the technique for measuring the durability of a part or material by subjecting it to a free fall, from a predetermined height onto a surface, under prescribed conditions. This test is a compulsory test for electronic goods, and helps ensure that components, fastenings and tolerances are appropriately robust.

The practical physical testing of products is a crucial aspect of a company's design, development and risk management strategy. Designers work closely with engineers during product testing to ensure that lessons learnt are fed back directly to the development team, designing in reliability and robustness. This is done, through the use of structured risk analysis tools, such as Failure Modes and Effects Analysis (FMEA), which enable the testing team to identify, quantify and mitigate the specific risks associated with product assemblies or individual components, and their proposed methods of manufacture. FMEA determines the location and nature of a failure, and whether a material defect contributed to the failure, helping the design team to understand and prevent future failures. Such analysis helps inform the development of a meticulously planned, conducted and documented testing regime, which can be used to investigate alternative design solutions, prove a particular design solution principle, investigate alternative design solutions or carry out specific robustness tests. During the design of most products and their constituent components, the expected physical stresses and loads the product will need to endure are determined, and these are used to design the required components and inform material selection.

Devising and running a well-controlled laboratory test rig evaluation, rather than relying on field evaluation, can lead to a much better understanding of the strength of a set of components, and can enable the iterative development of improved designs more rapidly than relying on field evaluation.

Fig. 6
Testing a chair using heavy weights to pound, bend and flex the chair through thousands of cycles to see how long it will take to fail.

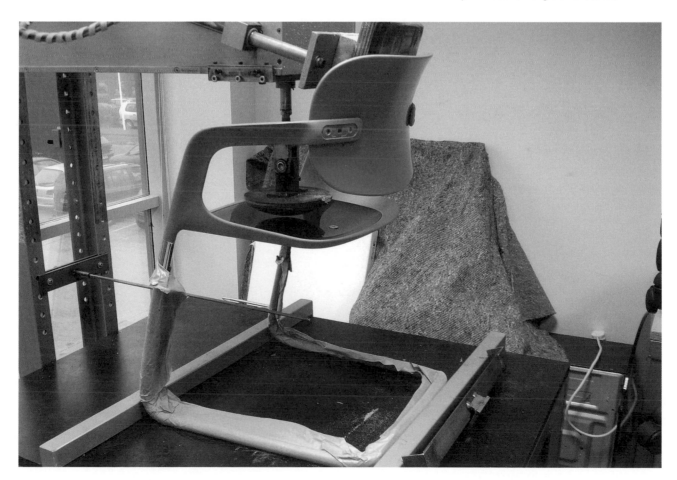

Fig. 7
Selection of international safety standard marks.
(Top to bottom) Conformité Européenne,
Canadian Standards Association, British
Standards Institution, BEAB (British
Electrotechnical Approvals Board), Germany's
TÜV mark and America's UK (Underwriters
Laboratories Ltd.).

Figs 8 & 9
(Opposite) Cars are subjected to the most
rigorous of tests. The images opposite show
seatbelt testing using crash test dummies, and
testing tyre skids in a controlled environment.

Safety testing

Product safety is a primary issue concern when designing, testing or, indeed,
purchasing a product. A product may be unsafe due to a fault in either the
manufacturing process or the design process. A fault in the manufacturing
process will lead to a product not functioning as it was designed to. For example,
the locks on a folding baby buggy may fail to engage properly when the buggy is
unfolded, causing it to collapse. Such safety faults can be identified through
extensive testing, and problems with the production quality, strength or tolerance
of components can then be resolved through production design changes.

A product may, however, have been manufactured as intended and function
properly but be unsafe due to a design defect. For example, a folding chair may
unlock unexpectedly when the user tries to move it, trapping their fingers. This
type of problem is usually due to a product being designed to meet a set of criteria
that fail to accurately reflect real-world conditions. This will then have been
compounded by the failure to pick up the problem, and the problem not having
been picked up in testing due to a lack of insufficient material and/or user testing.

Safety testing is an increasingly a key issue in determining consumer
purchasing decisions. A prime example of high-profile safety testing undertaken
today is the European New Car Assessment Programme (Euro NCAP). By law, all
new car models must pass certain safety tests before they are sold. However,
while this legislation provides a minimum statutory standard of safety for new cars,
it is the aim of the Euro NCAP tests to encourage manufacturers to exceed these
minimum requirements.

Current testing evaluates adult and child occupant protection, pedestrian
protection and how the latest safety-assistance technologies, such as anti-lock
brakes, really assist drivers. Euro NCAP publishes safety reports on new cars, and
awards 'star ratings' based on the performance of the vehicles in a variety of crash
tests, including front, side and pole impacts, and impacts with pedestrians. The
top overall rating is five stars, and this rating is now a key promotional device used
by manufacturers, and recognized by consumers, across Europe.

Product safety legislation provides a set of stringent test criteria that
products must pass before being put on sale. Such legislation has been
harmonized throughout international trade blocks such as the European Union to
ensure that less stringent requirements in one country cannot provide a back door
for unsafe products to reach another, and that over-stringent requirements in
some countries cannot be used to prevent the sale of perfectly safe products in
others. In the European Union, for example, products that comply with the
legislation are marked with the letters 'CE' (Conformité Européenne) – this logo
indicates to enforcement authorities that the manufacturer claims compliance with
the relevant local and international laws, and in many cases it is now illegal to sell
products at home or abroad that are not CE- marked. In the USA, UL
(Underwriters Laboratories Ltd.) is one of the main certifying bodies and the FM
Global and CSA (Canadian Standards Association) will also conduct testing but
these both have their own standards for testing products and the technique used
depends on the type of equipment and the volume.

Particular types of products are also subject to type testing. These tests may
be used by manufacturers during the design of their products but are principally
aimed at providing an independent third party, such as the UK's FIRA (Furniture
Industry Research Association), with a benchmark against which products can be
assessed comprehensively and fairly. Consumers in the UK would recognize the
BSI's (British Standards Institution) Kitemark and the Interek's BEAB Approved
Mark. In Europe the standard type test is the TÜV's GS Mark, while in the USA it is
the UL Mark. These tests and the results they produce are recognized both
nationally and internationally, and provide a vital safety net for consumers.

Case Study

MINI E all-electric car

Introduction

The MINI E project was the largest trial programme undertaken by a major car manufacturer to explore the day-to-day viability of an all-electric- powered car. Over a two-year testing process, starting in 2009 and involving users in big-city conurbations in California, Germany, France, Japan, China and the UK, more than 500 cars were deployed for private use. Based on the iconic MINI, the MINI E replaced the production car's petrol engine for an electric motor, and the rear seats with a large battery compartment.

Objective

The pilot project aimed to enable MINI, and its parent company BMW, to build up a representative picture of the market potential of all-electric cars.

Methods

The project adopted a user trials research approach, and aimed to develop a clear idea of the potential of electrically powered mobility in the everyday lives of consumers. It sought to provide answers to the following questions:

— Who will our prospective customers be?
— What requirements and expectations will they have?
— What share of the current market can be reached with electric vehicles?
— What kind of driving cycles and user profiles are we seeing in everyday conditions?

Environmentalists and early-adopters of technology were deliberately selected among the sample users, helping to promote silent urban transport, and position MINI and BMW as environmentally conscious brands.

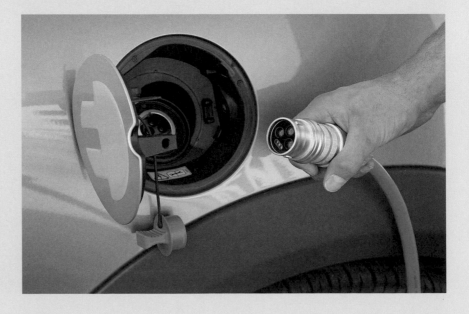

The Mini E was developed as a demonstration vehicle for BMW to test their new electric car technology.

Results

The company learnt invaluable lessons from the project. It provided real-world insights that complemented their abstract scenario testing, materials testing and questionnaires and surveys. MINI discovered the real-life effects of the new battery- powered vehicles' range restrictions, and how much of a problem these are for drivers. Customers also gave feedback on how they rated the experience of 'filling up' at home as opposed to visiting a petrol station, and how much value they placed on zero-emissions driving.

These findings have helped inform the corporate testing process, and led to the creation of Project i, BMW's new organizational unit, which deals with mobility issues and the needs of customers in the future. The next stage of the project focuses on the development of new vehicle concepts, (for production before 2015), such as the i8 sports car and the Megacity i3 electric car, designed to employ electric power and innovative lightweight carbon-fibre construction from inception.

After a successful global user-testing regime the Mini E formed part of the 2012 Olympic Games vehicle fleet.

Case Study

Berghaus Limpet system

Testing in extreme conditions is a vital element of the Berghaus development process.

Introduction

Berghaus began in 1966 when English climbers and mountaineers Peter Lockey and Gordon Davison, frustrated by what they saw as a lack of decent outdoor gear, decided to set up their own shop. The business soon became so successful that Lockey and Davison began to design, test and make their own gear for sale in the shop. This high-quality, innovative product range, inspired by what outdoor enthusiasts actually wanted and needed, was called Berghaus. Today, Berghaus is a global brand, selling products all over the world. The design team consists of a group of designers from different outdoor backgrounds, working on apparel, equipment and footwear.

Objective

Berghaus has always held a reputation for innovation within rucksack design, and they have sought to maintain this through the creation of radical new design solutions.

Methods

In 1998 the Nitro rucksack was launched, with its unique Limpet carry and compression system. It was awarded the Millennium product award by The Design Council of Great Britain. As part of a new range of lightweight packs, the Limpet system was developed into a range of namesake lightweight packs suitable for fast adventure adrenaline sports. The versatile range is designed to be used for hiking, mountain biking, climbing, and running. The ideology behind the Limpet system was to keep the pack stable on the wearers back by compressing the contents. Initially the designers began by talking to adventure racers, cyclists, and running sports enthusiasts about how they

move when carrying a rucksack. A number of prototypes were produced and tested by runners on their daily commute to see how the contents of their pack moved with them. This lead to further development of the Limpet system, enabling the packs to compress and stabilize the load on the a wearer's back while staying in sync with the complex movement of running. At this stage the designer has to be able to gain primary research into how the pack is working, crucial at this point because the users cannot always say what needs to be improved; the pack and its use has to be studied to understand where improvements can be made.

Once this new innovation was formed, the materials of the pack were chosen and subjected to materials testing to make sure they meet Berghaus' standard requirements. Each feature was carefully considered against human factors, weight, and durability. They were first individually tested in the in-house Berghaus lab, and then field-tested in the conditions in which the rucksack will be used. The Berghaus lab test materials and components against high standards of hydrostatic head, abrasion, spray testing, tear strength, yarn configuration, weight, and colour fastness for light, washing, and perspiration. Once the components have passed the stringent testing, they are then made into a rucksack. Prototypes were produced of the design of the rucksack and sent to an external testing company for field testing. This involved a company called Klets, who field test the prototypes for a minimum of 200 hours, to see noting where if any material or human factor weaknesses would emerge in the design. After the prototype has

developed further, it is then tested by the Berghaus Athletes to make sure it meets their high demands.

Results

Rigorous testing, combined with cutting-edge technologies and manufacturing techniques, enabled the Berghaus designers to achieve a crucial reduction in weight, as well as an improvement in load transfer, movement and comfort. The thorough testing of outdoor gear only enhances the capabilities the product.

Products are subjected to a rigorous series of usability tests in the field.

Case Study

Building a test rig: PearsonLloyd's DBO commode

Sketch models are a vital part of the development process, and enable designers to refine the physical and ergonomic qualities of a product

Introduction

Designers strive to create products that satisfy the needs and desires of their intended users. However, to ensure they are aware of what the actual, rather than perceived, needs are, they must put their designs through a comprehensive ergonomic testing procedure. Designers know that intuitive, easy-to-operate products are satisfying to use, but many products still place unnecessarily high physical demands on users, or exclude some altogether; from older people and the disabled to economically vulnerable groups and those affected by changing technologies and work practices.

Ergonomic test rigs are an essential design development tool in the successful creation of inclusive products – products that can be used and accessed by as many members of society as reasonably possible. When creating an ergonomic test rig you should start by basing your rig on the appropriate anthropometric data to establish the basic dimensions of the rig. You should design the rig to be easily re-configurable to allow a range of different options to be trialled and evaluated. Extensive studies can then be arranged to record and analyze the interaction of a representative user group with the rigs, and this data, combined with existing research data, will help towards the design of ergonomically sound inclusive products.

Ergonomic test rigs may be small, hand-held block models that are used to evaluate product form and the operation of user controls and displays, in products such as mobile phones. Or they may be representative of larger industrial equipment and used to check user interfaces, comfort and physical demands. Ergonomic test rigs are also used to evaluate transportation or architectural interiors, to monitor sight lines, seating and access. However, they are most commonly used by designers when developing furniture or seating, to help evaluate seat heights, rake and lumbar support. A prime example of their use can be seen in Pearson Lloyd's project.

Objective

This project aimed to address the problems surrounding the ergonomic, hygienic and psychological issues surrounding hospital commodes. Existing commodes tended to be made up of multiple parts, with complex junctions between different materials. This makes it difficult and time-consuming to take them apart for thorough cleaning, and increases the risk of infection.

Methods

PearsonLloyd used an intensive series of product usability testing to developed a radical design that proposed a simplified construction that would makes cleaning the commode quicker and easier, reducing the risk of hospital infections. Functional and aesthetic changes also improved patient comfort and dignity. Instead of mounting the pan on the underside of the seat, the ergonomic testing they undertook led to the design of a top-loading system for the pan. This helped eliminate gaps and openings, preventing waste from contaminating hard-to-reach parts of the commode.

Results

With fewer touch-points of contact between patient and commode, the final design dramatically reduces the chance of cross-infection through contact with contaminated surfaces. A detachable plastic shell and robust stainless steel frame make the commode easy to clean and easy to store. The commode has adjustable armrests so patients can slide directly onto it from a bed or chair, and adjustable footrests to help patients to get into and out of the commode. User testing of existing commodes on the market led to an invaluable insight: users felt that they looked like a piece of furniture, an aesthetic that patients found deeply inappropriate in the context of a hospital. The new design deliberately resembles a toilet instead of a domestic armchair, which helps to put patients at ease when using it at the bedside.

This project has been widely promoted as a great example of how to design for wellbeing and healthcare. The design is easier and cheaper to manufacture than existing products on the market, and has under testing demonstrated lower levels of infection under testing.

PearsonLloyd explored a range of materials and forms when developing their user-centred commode. The final version, shown here, is top-loading and has a stainless steel frame and moulded polypropylene components.

How to run a great user trial

In order to run a successful user trial you should take the following steps:

Set goals

When undertaking user trials you need to determine the key issues you wish to explore in order to provide useful design feedback. You may also need to set criteria, such as acceptable levels of performance and error rates in order to determine whether the product under test meets usability metrics targets.

Design your test

You should decide on the number of users to be involved – the larger the sample, the more representative the test. Provided that detailed comparisons are not required, five test participants is usually sufficient. If the test involves more than one product or system, you must be clear whether the same user should be tested using both/all of them, or tested using only one. Testing participants with the same tasks on two different products or systems risks the results being affected by a potential transfer of experience between the two products under test. When evaluating the subjective preferences of users, it is best to let users test all the products.

Write a procedure plan

This describes how the test will be run from start to finish, and how it will be observed, filmed and recorded. It prescribes the sequence of tasks to be performed, when and what questions are asked, and how instructions are given. The procedure plan should also describe how the observations are to be made. You should pay strict attention to the logistics and scheduling of trials to avoid users having to sit and wait or being asked to come back another time.

Pilot the test

It is a good idea to run pilot trials with easily available subjects such as colleagues until you are sure that there will be no technical and procedural problems during the testing. It is important that the tasks are representative of the product under consideration. One approach is to try to select tasks that will be performed frequently by a typical user, although emphasis should also be placed on those tasks that are particularly important, such as safety.

Pre-test interviews and questionnaires

Before the actual testing, the users should be interviewed for relevant background information, such as age and gender. You should also find out if they have any prior experience with similar products.

Put your users at ease

You should allow sufficient time to introduce the users to the activities required. Try to ensure that the tests last, ideally, no longer than an hour to ensure users are unaffected by tiredness or other distractions. It is also extremely important that the testing and interviewing are performed in a relaxed and friendly atmosphere, where the user does not feel anxious. Avoid criticizing the user in any way for their performance, and emphasize that it is the product rather than the person that is being evaluated.

Post-test interviews

Once the test is complete you should interview the users to capture invaluable feedback. During the interviews, the user's attention should be directed towards the product, and not towards their own shortcomings or failings in operating the product. You should also allow sufficient time to conclude the interview session, by answering any questions that participants may have.

Data analysis

A list of problems and issues is the usual output of a user trial, and these should be ranked in order of severity by the users. This might be done by asking users or experts to rate each problem on a ten-point scale. If this is not possible, you should rank the problems according to your own judgement.

Learning from the test

Once you have analyzed the data, you should determine how this can be used to inform your design processes and improve your product. Your video recording of the test and the problems identified is a particularly powerful communication tool, and can demonstrate more effectively than words to colleagues, clients and stakeholders, the practical problems experienced by end-users when operating equipment.

Trialing a hand-held game. It is important when conducting a user trial that you gain feedback on durability and practicality as well as aesthetic qualities.

EVALUATION
& SELECTION

Choosing the right methods

Designers need reliable, rigorous and robust methods of evaluating and selecting their design proposals. Selecting the wrong product design proposal to develop can be very costly to manufacturers and stakeholders in terms of time, money and other valuable resources, so there is a major incentive for designers to get their evaluations and selections right first time. Evaluating and selecting concept design proposals is a convergent process and it is frequently highly iterative.

Choosing the right methods is, therefore, extremely important. Developing and launching new products carries risk: Will it appeal to the target market? Does it have the right features? Can it be manufactured profitably? Is the development cost justified? It is no longer safe for product designers to react to risks as they develop; instead, designers must actively identify and measure these risks before they become a problem. In order to effectively track and manage the risk associated with delivering innovation, design companies, no matter how small, should develop a robust risk management strategy or face potentially disastrous consequences.

Designers are constantly evaluating which directions to take while, at the same time, generating many concepts to choose from. The systematic evaluation techniques presented in this chapter should help maximize your chances of selecting the right design proposal. When considering a proposal it is helpful to draw up a product design specification (PDS), which is essential during the design process and also clearly sets out the parameters which must be met so the designer can make an informed decision before taking on a project. Below are some of the key points that should appear in a PDS.

Product Design Specification

1. Performance
2. Environment
3. Life in service
4. Maintenance
5. Target product cost
6. Competition
7. Packing
8. Shipping/transport
9. Quality
10. Manufacturing facility
11. Size
12. Weight
13. Aesthetics
14. Materials
15. Product life span
16. Standards/specifications
17. Ergonomics
18. Customer
19. Quality and reliability
20. Shelf life storage
21. Processes
22. Timescale
23. Testing
24. Safety
25. Company constraints
26. Market constraints
27. Patents
28. Political/social implications
29. Legal considerations
30. Installation
31. Documentation
32. Disposal

(Opposite page) Sofia Lagerkvist, Charlotte von der Lancken and Anna Lindgren of Swedish design group Front.

Fig. 1
The PDS is a dynamic document that can, and often does, change over the course of the design process. The PDS should lay out the main considerations of a brief at the beginning of a project.

Fig. 2

A typical product checklist. The use of such lists helps designers ensure they meet the challenge of addressing all of the issues raised in the product design specification (PDS).

Product 'Z' Checklist

Product materials must resist corrosion. ☒

All fixings must comply with International Standards. ☒

Target manufacturing cost is no higher than £15.00. ☒

Weight of the product must not exceed 10kg (22lb). ☐

Design process must be completed by 4 July. ☒

Manufacturing sign off no later than 12 September. ☐

Delivery of first product no later than 14 January. ☒

'Z' logo clearly seen on product. ☒

Checklists

A checklist is a very useful device, particularly when it comes to alleviating or eliminating any errors that might arise in the design and development of products, services, systems or environments. Sometimes referred to as 'to do' lists, checklists make tasks or objectives that need to be met explicit. This is especially useful when designing products and services that have a high degree of interaction with the end-user. Checklists can also help ensure consistency and completeness in carrying out specific tasks and are commonly found in a number of areas, such as the aerospace industry, healthcare, engineering, and in projects with potentially significant public liability issues.

Generally speaking, the product design specification (PDS) can be viewed as a form of checklist. In product design projects, a PDS is created to ensure that the product designer produces a design solution that reflects a true understanding of the actual problem and the needs of the user. In short, the PDS is a series of checklists split into smaller categories to make it easier to consider. These might cover categories such as cost, safety, size, packaging and quantity, and include specific requirements such as:

— The product's cost of manufacture must be no higher than £3.00 per unit.
— The length of the product should be no greater than 75 mm or 3 inches.
— The weight of the product must be kept to a minimum and no greater than 1.5 kilograms.
— The product must be waterproof.

A checklist is not a set of instructions – its aim is to help identify and address common problems and errors during specific stages of the design and development of a new product. For this reason, it should be simple, measurable and translatable. A checklist is also a good tool for managing actions and communications between members of the design and development team. Generally speaking, the checklist is meant to be read aloud as actions are being performed: 'The product's cost of manufacture is less than £3.00 per unit' – 'CHECK!', and so on. A checklist should be seen as a dynamic document that evolves over the course of the design process as elements are tested, re-tested and refined.

Fig. 3
Designers seek to verify their concepts through
discussion with stakeholders, evaluating their
concepts' respective merits, and refining their
designs through invaluable user input.

External decision making

Designers are increasingly looking to engage consumers and stakeholders in the
design process, and involve customers and clients in the decision-making
process. When designing 'with' rather than 'for' people, there is a spectrum of
engagement that a design team can operate within:

— Stakeholder consultation is the minimum level of engagement generally
  acceptable in practice today, with users informing and influencing the decision
  making through methods such as focus groups, surveys and questionnaires.
— Participatory design actively involves people at all stages of the design
  process to ensure their concerns are understood and considered, and to give
  them some influence on and ownership of design decisions. This level of
  engagement requires a greater level of dialogue with the stakeholders, and
  often takes the form of inclusive design workshops, where participants can
  actually shape the design process.
— Collaborative design brings people into an active design partnership and the
  designers and stakeholders agree a full and frank sharing of resources and
  decision making. Examples of this approach include companies setting up
  advisory panels and strategic partnerships with a range of stakeholders.
— Design delegation is the most extreme intensity of engagement, where a
  manufacturer delegates the design decision-making process to consumers,
  through the use of methods such as ballots and referendums. This apparently
  democratic model relies on the questions being asked of the ' voters' being
  carefully written and designed to ensure clarity of purpose, and an explicit
  description of how any decisions will be subsequently implemented.

Involving large numbers of users in the evaluation and selection of designs
undoubtedly provides invaluable feedback and insights to the design team, but
this can sometimes be impossible due to time or financial constraints. As such,
it is common practice to try to gain useful feedback from a number of diverse
representative users and stakeholders to reduce biases in the sample users'
responses and observations.

The following list can help to structure your use of external decision making:
— Broad user mix – this involves users from a range of market segments, which can help understand general user requirements.
— Boundary users – this involves users on the limit of being able to use the product, which can help identify opportunities for design improvement.
— Extreme users – these can inspire creativity during concept development.
— Mixed-experience users – those with different levels of experience with similar products can help understand the impact of experience on use.
— Community groups – again, those sharing experience of interacting with similar products can provide a broad understanding of product use.

Intuition

A product designer's intuition can be an important factor in the evaluation and selection of concept design proposals. A decision based on intuition alone is where a concept is chosen for its 'feel', with the designers relying on their own tacit knowledge rather than explicit criteria. When product designers are asked to articulate their skills and explain how they work and make decisions, 'personal intuition' is one of the most frequently given responses.

Design intuition is an important and effective part of a designer's make-up. It takes years of experience and practice to hone, and depends on careful observation of people, the products they use and how they use them. A designer might not always be able to articulate their judgements and decision making analytically, but this does not necessarily indicate that their intuitions are weak. In practice, product design projects proceed by a combination of intuition and reasoned analysis.

Intuition is a difficult concept to define but one that most designers recognize as crucial. It is not strictly speaking a methodology, although when matched with play, it can influence your creativity, and shape your personal design methodology. Play is an unavoidable and essential element in the design process, but one which is largely ignored. The dry, reductivist view of design that seeks to promote the designer as an objective, emotionless entity struggles when looking for explanations of recent design trends, such as the playful designs of Alessi and Droog Design's 'Do' collection. The psychologist Carl Jung tells us: 'The creation of something new is not accomplished by the intellect but by the play instinct acting from inner necessity. The creative mind plays with the objects it loves.' This argument seems fairly natural and familiar to most practicing designers, although the intuitive and play element of their work may be 'underplayed' in their professional lives.

There are several kinds of intuition – the intuition of the product designer is unlike that of the engineer, and both will be dissimilar to the marketing specialist. The role and nature of intuition in design has been somewhat overlooked by many design writers and critics, perhaps because it is one of many unobservable mental entities that scientists are yet to completely understand. For designers, intuition relies heavily on insights that are based on both knowledge and experience.

The key conditions necessary for intuition appear to be:
— Sufficient conceptual knowledge and experience of the field.
— A strong motivation to resolve the issues associated with the project.
— A period of relaxation, when the designer is not consciously thinking about the project. This might include listening to music, falling asleep or awakening.

To paraphrase Thomas Alva Edison's famous quote – great inventions are 1 per cent intuition (inspiration) and 99 per cent perspiration. Intuition in design can often lead to brilliant ideas quickly. On the other hand, it can be extremely unreliable both in terms of time and usefulness. The main problem with relying on intuition alone is that it might never happen.

Fig. 4
(Opposite) Designer Max Lamb takes a very hands-on and intuitive approach to design. His pieces have materials and process at their heart, and achieve a rawness and sense of craftsmanship that machined products just don't have. Seen here is the process of creating his Urushi Stool using primitive green-woodworking techniques.

Crowdsourcing

The term crowdsourcing was first coined by Jeff Howe in a June 2006 *Wired* magazine article, where he stated that new technologies and communication platforms such as the internet enabled companies to take advantage of the expertise of the public, and involve them in the creative design and decision-making process. Howe stated that 'It's not outsourcing; it's crowdsourcing.'

Crowdsourcing is essentially the act of outsourcing tasks traditionally performed by experts to a group of people through an online open call. The idea is that actively engaging people outside the usual corporate environment can access a far larger pool of expertise, who can perform tasks, solve complex problems and contribute fresh ideas. Companies are eager to find new insights, ideas for new products and qualitative inspiration from their users, and a dedicated community crowdsourcing platform can be the perfect tool with which to start the conversation with their target group.

Crowdsourcing can take a variety of forms, but the usual format is for a company to present a new product concept to their online community. This community of users, experts and interested parties is then able to freely modify the current design or upload their own ideas, using any combination of comments, sketches, pictures, mood boards, movies, prototypes or total redesigns. Rewards for inputs can range from a payment or entry into a competition, through to a formal royalties deal for a chosen design.

The ideas and comments generated online are fed back to the company's research and development team who then use this data to inform their decision making. The hoped-for result is the co-creation of products that are better aligned with what their consumers really want.

Fig. 5
Companies are increasingly engaging the general public in the development of their products through methods such as crowdsourcing, where large groups' opinions are gathered or they are asked to trial a particular topic.

A recent development has been the introduction of crowdvoting, which makes use of the power of popular opinion to rank and sort all kinds of data. Often this interaction takes place in real time, with companies promoting their brand or product through live content. By asking large numbers of potential consumers to vote for a particular concept over another, companies are able to generate significant levels of consumer interest and buy-in for the winning concept that enters production. This form of crowdsourcing is increasingly used as a marketing tool, alongside other forms of social media, such as Facebook and Twitter, to develop and promote new products.

Recent examples of the use of social media to develop or promote products include Vitamin Water and Fiorelli. Vitamin Water asked users on their Facebook page to help them choose the next flavour of the drink to be released and effectively crowdsourced their creative design process. The campaign was endorsed and supported by leading celebrities and created a considerable online trend on Twitter. Luxury accessories brand Fiorelli recently launched a presence on Facebook that included a new social shopping experience for customers and fans. Buying an expensive Fiorelli bag is a major investment for most customers. The brand have taken this into consideration by introducing a Facebook app that allows people to superimpose a photo of their bag of choice onto their profile photo and receive their friends' comments before they decide to purchase, thus demonstrating the use of social media to help influence customers' actual purchasing journey.

Product champions

Many people would argue that a product champion is absolutely crucial for any company designing and developing new products today. A product champion is an influential member of the new product design and development team. She or he supports the instigation and development of concept design proposals that, in turn, help determine the overall design direction. The importance of product champions to the success of developing innovative products was highlighted in business and management research in the 1960s, and decades of studies since have supported these claims. A product champion is seen **as a** vital cog in the innovation process – needed to overcome organizational barriers and resistance within companies. Several proponents believe that new product design ideas either find a champion or die.

The role of a product champion, essentially, is to actively and enthusiastically promote and sell a project in order to obtain vital and valuable organizational resources and support. Moreover, product champions are individuals who might

Fig. 6
Brands regularly employ product champions to evaluate and promote their products, and an endorsement from a leading sports star such as Lionel Messi can guarantee commercial success.

occasionally have to take personal risks by advocating and demonstrating the feasibility of a project to reluctant top management.

The product champion acts as an important go-between or linkage point between various departments within an organization. He or she will possess good knowledge of the organization's capabilities and resources and will know which individuals should be concerned with the innovation, thus connecting the organization's sponsor(s) with the internal and perhaps external experts. One of the product champion's key strengths will be the ability to translate the technical language of an innovation into terminology that is commonly used in the organization – for example, they will ensure management and business leaders within the company are able to understand the work of the design and engineering team. By becoming a salesman of a new design idea, the product champion is able to develop a plan of action, using their diplomatic talents to provide access to different people within the organization.

Matrix evaluation

Matrix evaluation, sometimes referred to as 'Pugh's Method' after the British engineering design professor Stuart Pugh, is a quantitative technique used by designers to evaluate their concept design proposals by ranking them against the set criteria stated in the product design specification (PDS) and/or against other concept design proposals. While many stages involved in the product design and development process benefit from unrestrained creativity and divergent thinking, the selection of concept design proposals is the process of narrowing down a number of alternative proposals to select one for further development and refinement.

This is a convergent process, but it is frequently iterative and may not produce a strong or dominant concept proposal immediately. The matrix evaluation technique may have to be run several times before a strong concept design proposal emerges as ripe for further development. Thus, selection and evaluation are iterative processes that must be embedded in the development of new products.

Decision matrix model (Pugh's Method)

— Select decision criteria
— Formulate decision matrix
— Clarify design concepts being evaluated
— Choose datum or best initial concept
— Compare other concepts to datum based on a +, –, S scale
— Evaluate the ratings; discuss concept's strengths and weaknesses
— Select a new datum concept and re-run analysis
— Plan further work
— Second working session to repeat above steps and select a concept

Designers constantly evaluate and select which direction to take while generating design proposals. Typically, this will mean that several concept design proposals need to be chosen from. Usually, with matrix evaluation, a large number of proposals will be rapidly narrowed down to a more concise and focused number. This might involve combining specific features of one concept with another totally different concept to improve and temporarily enlarge the set of concepts being evaluated and selected. Eventually, after working through several iterations, a dominant concept proposal will emerge.

When selecting which concept design proposals best satisfy the PDS, it is essential to remember the need to generate wholly new concepts, adapt existing ones or undertake further research to proceed. Evaluation and selection should be a narrowing process, weeding out unsuitable ideas, rather than trying to pick the 'best idea'. Referring back to the PDS and placing yourself in the user's position can help avoid selection on a purely subjective basis.

Once an appropriate number of design concepts have been generated through sketching and modelling, the design team can refer back to the PDS and evaluate and select which concepts fulfil the criteria laid out in the original specification. To avoid subjectivity and personal intuition creeping into the decision-making process, it is imperative that all members of the product design and development team perform this vital part of the process. If possible, input should also be included from the client and/or stakeholders, helping to evaluate and select the concept design proposals outlined from a number of perspectives. Matrix evaluation can help designers, engineers, manufacturers, marketing staff, users, clients and buyers to reduce ambiguity and confusion in the evaluation and selection process, enjoy better communication, and deliver successful new products to market more rapidly.

Fig. 7
Evaluation matrices are used to evaluate a number of design options against prioritized criteria. This process is relatively simple to apply and aids the design team in making objective decisions.

Criteria

Concepts

	▲	⬠	●	◯	☐	
Product materials must resist corrosion	+	-	+	=	=	
All fixings must comply with International Standards	+	=	-	+	=	D
Target manufacturing cost is no higher than £15.00	+	+	=	=	-	A
Weight of the product must not exceed 10kg (22lb)	=	=	-	+	+	T
Design process must be completed by 4 July	+	+	+	=	=	U
Manufacturing sign off no later than 12 September	=	=	=	-	-	M
Delivery of first product no later than 14 January	=	-	=	=	-	
'Z' logo clearly seen on the product	=	-	=	=	-	
Totals	4+ 0- 4=	2+ 3- 2+	2+ 2- 4=	2+ 1- 5=	1+ 4- 3=	

Case Study

Seren: downloadable service design

Seren offer a complete range of design services, including research, strategy, product and service design, app development, UX and visual design, analytics and innovation.

Introduction

Seren is an independent design consultancy based in Shoreditch, London. Seren designs interactive services and builds brands by connecting research, insight and innovation to design using different tools and methodologies, such as personas, perceptual mapping and user narration:

— Personas: identifying customers and what matters to them
— Perceptual mapping: linking corporate goals to measures
— User narration: mapping journeys across channels

This approach enables the company to understand the subtle, multi-channel relationship between users and brands and thereby design meaningful experiences.

Objective

Orange was looking to make mobile communication more natural and intuitive, and chose to work with Seren to develop ON – a free, downloadable service that lets users communicate differently with the people who matter, just as they do in person. ON brings together all contacts (and communications) from a mobile, Twitter, Facebook and email into one meaningful phone book. Users then make decisions on what to share with whom – and how – according to their relationship with them.

In 2009 Seren began working closely with Orange Vallée (Orange's innovation division) and a branding agency, to help create a powerful brand position for ON. The overall experience strategy was developed based on the brand values of 'gracious', 'elegant', 'real' and 'alive'.

Methods

To inform the service design, Seren adopted a number of crowdsourcing techniques, including research tools such as guerrilla testing, interactive prototyping and mental mapping. These provided insights into the mental models of users, and how those mental models changed depending on a user's situation and the task they were performing. For example, they explored whether users thought of a contextual voicemail and then formed a group around that, or whether they organized contacts into a group and then created a certain voicemail for them. The aim was to offer a service that truly had users at its heart – an important perspective that many similar services (such as Google+, the Facebook Timeline) and organizations strive to follow.

Results

Continual research on different facets of the service pushed Seren to ensure that as it developed, the overall design really delivered ON's brand values. Insight informed the interface design, from the sequence of screens to the placement of information on those screens. ON went live in December 2011, first on Android, then on iPhone, and has now been developed across desktop computers. It continues to reflect the changing ways people stay in tune with their complex personal networks.

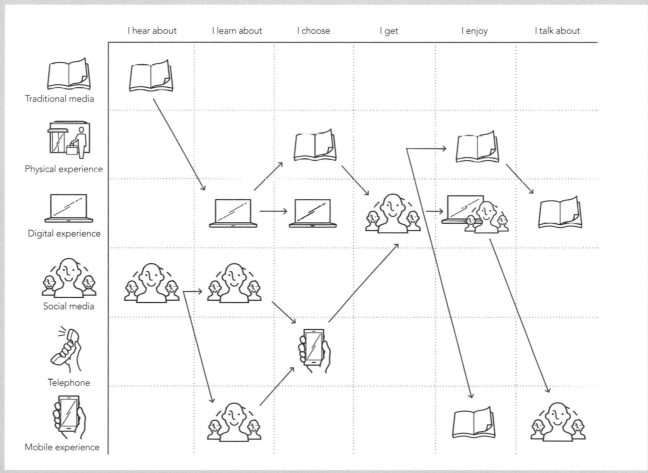

Seren developed On for Orange. On is a free, downloadable application that reflects the way people interact. It automatically pieces together information from diverse sources to compile a single 'version' of each of your contacts that is secure and backed up. At the same time, it lets you categorize those contacts so you can present a subtly different face to people, depending on how well and in what context you know them. Seren's approach to service design means that On reflects the brand values of Orange. Every time a customer uses it they experience its personal, straightforward, honest nature.

Case Study

Land Rover
DC100 Defender

Introduction

For more than six decades, Land Rover has been designing and building 4x4s that define capability, versatility and usability – none more so than their iconic Defender. These vehicles have, over the years, been put to every task and reconfigured in every way, from fire engines to tracked exploration vehicles, and an estimated three-quarters of the nearly two million Defenders built are still in regular use.

Objective

Land Rover prepared the launch of two concepts – the DC100 and the DC100 Sport –to build on the essential and intuitive elements of the Defender's character. John Edwards, Global Brand Director of Land Rover, explained their intention to 'engage with existing and potential customers to help us finalize the details of the new vehicle'.

Methods

The classic Land Rover features were retained – short front and rear overhangs, four-square stance, a high 'command' driving position and superb ground clearance. Sketching, sketch modelling and appearance modelling were used to design a simple exterior surface language, with a strong shoulder running the full length of the vehicle and defining the corners. A sense of space was created for the interior with a low centre console and three-abreast seating.

The intuitive design has an inherent flexibility – for example, the central instruments can be removed from the vehicle and used outside for continued 'on foot' navigation or to capture remote explorations on film, through inbuilt cameras.

This combination of go-anywhere capability and adaptability openly invites existing owners and prospective buyers to actively engage in the design development process, while also retaining the open, honest character and timeless simplicity of the original.

Results

Defender became a global icon because of the integrity of both its design and engineering. In creating these concepts Land Rover took the functional design cues from the past and reinterpreted them for the 21st century. The reception to the concepts has been largely positive, and Land Rover will continue to develop the design for production through intensive online questionnaires and surveys, focus groups and user testing across the globe, through to the launch of a new Defender in 2015.

Full size clay modelling is still a key part of the design process, ensuring a product's formal and tactile delight.

(Clockwise from top left) Development sketches aim to capture the essence of a product. The concepts are evaluated at events by selected audiences comprising of potential buyers, model enthusiasts and expert journalists. The DC100 references the iconic original Land Rover from 1948. Land Rover explore the bandwidth of their brand through presenting extreme versions of their concepts, to test market acceptance. The interior aesthetic and ergonomics form a vital part of the Land Rover DNA.

How to conduct a matrix evaluation

Matrix evaluation is a reliable tool for structuring the evaluation and selection of concept design proposals. To evaluate concepts effectively, an agreed set of criteria – perhaps a checklist or PDS (see the next tutorial) – is required. Matrix evaluation is best carried out with a small group, although it can also be conducted as an individual activity.

The 14-step matrix evaluation procedure is as follows:

1. All of the concept design proposals must be generated to fulfil the same criteria set out in the PDS or checklist.

2. All of the concept design proposals must be represented to the same level of detail, be that in sketch or 3D model form.

3. Create a concept evaluation and selection matrix that will facilitate comparison of the generated concept design proposals against the criteria and one another.

4. It is important that the matrix includes all of the concept proposal visuals (e.g. sketches, models) so that the team can observe the pattern of evaluation that emerges. Textual descriptions of the concept proposals may be added to increase clarity.

5. The criteria that the concept design proposals are to be evaluated against must be defined before the generation of solutions begins. The criteria must be stated in unambiguous terms and understood and accepted by all members of the design team involved in the evaluation and selection process.

6. Select one concept design proposal as the datum point against which the rest of the proposals will be compared. Usually this is the concept proposal that the team thinks is the 'best'.

7. Each concept/criteria pair must be compared against the datum proposal and the following symbols should be used:
   + (plus sign): means better than, less prone to, easier than, etc. the datum.
   – (minus sign): means worse than, more expensive then, more prone to, more difficult than, etc. the datum.
   = (equal sign): means the same as the datum.

8. After selecting the datum, make an initial comparison of the concept design proposals using the +, – and = symbols. A score pattern will be created for each proposal relative to the datum. Bear in mind that the numbers, at this stage, are for guidance only.

9. Assess the individual concept design proposal scores, paying particular attention to each proposal's strengths and weaknesses.

10. Next, assess the negatives of the strong concepts and see if they can be easily reversed into positives. At this stage, you might wish to expand the matrix by introducing modified concepts.

	●	▲	◆	⬟	◣	✚	☾	✤
	1	2	3	4	5	6	7	8
Withstand vandalism		+	=			-		
Not heavier than 2.5 kg		-	-			+		
Comply with the Home Safety Act (UK)		-	+			+		
Cost no more than £25.00		-	+			+		
100% recyclable		=	+			+		
Lasts 3 years minimum		-	+			-		
+ number		1	4	2	2	4	3	3
- number		4	1	3	4	2	3	2
= number		1	1	1	0	0	0	1

11. Similarly, explore the weak concepts now and see if their negatives can be improved upon (relative to the datum concept). If they can be improved upon then include them and expand the matrix.

12. After completing steps 10 and 11, the weak concepts should be eliminated from the matrix. This will reduce the matrix size.

13. If a number of strong concept design proposals do not emerge after conducting steps 10, 11 and 12 then it usually means one or two things:
— The criteria are ambiguous and are being interpreted differently by the design team, leading to confusion.
— Some of the concept proposals are either too similar in nature or even the same thing.

14. Once a strong concept proposal emerges, repeat the matrix evaluation using the strong concept as the datum. If the results are repeated it confirms the strength of the concept. If not, then repeat steps 10 and 11 until strong concepts emerge.

Having completed the 14 steps of the matrix evaluation listed above, the design team will have acquired:
— A sound insight into the requirements of the PDS or checklist.
— A better understanding of the problem or issues.
— A better insight into potential design solutions.
— A good knowledge of the strengths and weaknesses of the concept design proposals made.
— Greater motivation to produce other concept design proposals.

The above diagram shows a matrix evaluation using sample criteria.

How to write a checklist (PDS)

PDS/Checklist	
Performance	Ergonomics
Environment	Customer
Life in service	Quality and reliability
Maintenance	Shelf life storage
Target product cost	Processes
Competition	Timescale
Packing	Testing
Shipping/Transport	Safety
Quantity	Company constraints
Manufacturing facility	Market constraints
Size	Patents
Weight	Political/Social implications
Aesthetics	Legal
Materials	Installation
Product life span	Documentation
Standards/Specifications	Disposal

As stated earlier in this chapter, the product design specification (PDS) can be seen as a form of checklist. Typically, this created is as a written document that can be changed over the course of the design process (and usually is). Usually, the design of the product, service or environment will follow the statements laid out in the PDS. However, if the emerging design departs from the PDS for some good reason, then the PDS can be revised to accommodate the change. The important thing is to keep the PDS and the product being designed in correspondence throughout the design process. In this way, the PDS ends up specifying not just the design, but the product itself.

A comprehensive PDS will comprise a sequence of anything up to 32 categories that cover aspects of the intended product's performance, its cost, how it will be made, what it must look like and how it will be disposed of after its life in service. You should start writing your PDS by listing the 32 headings shown on the left.

PDS/Checklist	
Headings	**Elements**
Environment	The product should be able to withstand vandalism
Weight	The weight of the product should be no greater than 2.5 kg
Safety	The product must comply with all relevant parts of BS 3456 and the Home Safety Act (UK)
Target product cost	The retail cost of the product must be no higher than £25.00
Installation	The product must be ready assembled and not require user assembly for use

Next, you need to write the individual checklist elements under each of the 32 headings, leaving out only those that clearly do not apply. Some of the elements in the PDS/checklist will overlap, but do not be tempted to skip any of them. In some rare projects, however, it may be appropriate to leave out a number of elements as they may not be relevant, but this needs to be agreed by all the design project stakeholders in advance.

Every single PDS element should be written with a metric and a value. For example, 'The length (time) in service of product A' is a metric and 'No less than five years' is the value of this metric. Values should always be labelled with an appropriate unit (e.g. seconds, metres, kilograms). Both the metrics and the values form the basis of the PDS/checklist. The headings and elements shown here give an example of how you should complete your own checklist.

It should be emphasized, however, that the PDS/checklist spells out in precise, measurable detail what the product has to do but not how it should be done. Each PDS/checklist element should be clear and succinct, using short, sharp precise statements under each heading using metrics and values against each one.

COMMUNICATING

Communicating effectively with clients, collaborators, manufacturers and end-users is a vital core skill for any designer. It is crucial that you are able to communicate your ideas and thoughts to the other people involved in a design project by the use of design sketches, prototypes, presentation models or more formal oral presentations. Good communication is essential to successful product design projects, and engaging your clients, stakeholders and the general public in your work. This extends to the manner in which you present your work, how you present yourself, what you say and how you act. The following methods provide a number of ways to develop your presentation skills, from preparing a presentation to writing reports and maximizing the impact of presentation visuals and models.

Preparing a presentation

The manner, style and procedure in which an individual designer researches and develops a design concept can often be quite distinctive and personal. It involves the internal thinking process and external drawing and prototyping processes, and so is necessarily a complex journey, often taking a non-linear route from A to B as a designer grapples with new research information, visual realizations of concepts and feedback from colleagues, clients and users. As a result, presenting the design development process in a clear and logical manner can be challenging. However, a designer must to be able to present his or her development work – and make explicit the concepts and reasoning behind certain design evaluations and decisions – in order to communicate effectively with others, both within and outside the studio. Common strategies to achieve this include keeping sketchbooks, research folders and journals, which can be edited on a rolling basis to provide evidence and justification for the decisions taken. These help form the foundation for preparing your presentation visuals.

Always try to arrive at a presentation five or ten minutes in advance, and aim to finish on time; don't attempt to say too much and then leave yourself with the need either to rush through or go over the suggested limit. Over the page are ten top tips for a great presentation.

Fig. 1
Regular presentations within the design team ensure a smooth design development process.

Ten tips for a great presentation

1. Structure your presentation
Move from the particular to the general before returning to the particular. Offer the viewer an immediate pay-off for listening – a 'visual hook' that will catch the audience's attention and demonstrate what the concept of the project is early on (usually on the first or second page). Generalize – don't go into every detail of everything you've done, just select the important parts and highlight those.

2. Show examples
Show visual examples throughout the presentation to demonstrate your concept.

3. Provide a take-away
It's useful to give people something to take away with them after a presentation, so they remember what the work was about and who you are. It is a good idea to supplement your presentation with handouts such as a postcard, a booklet or a small sample sheet.

4. Show models
If your proposal or aspects of your design and development work have involved 3D models and/or props, then have these with you so that they can be handed around while you are talking to the audience.

5. Never assume anything
Always expect that the audience does not know what is in your head and find a simple, effective way to talk them through the design project.

6. Avoid being too formal
You don't need to be overly formal to get your message across. Try to speak at a 'colleague' level of intelligence and in an approachable but professional style.

7. Sequence your presentation
Your presentation, and how you talk an audience through your project, should generally follow the following sequence:
— State the main problem/question/aim
— Show evidence of that problem and the need for the outcome
— Outline the development of a solution and the approach you've taken
— Provide the solution

8. Non-verbal communication
Non-verbal communication is as important as what you say and what's on the presentation sheets. Smile when talking, and look at who you're presenting to. This communicates enthusiasm and develops a rapport with the audience so that even if you forget the words or stumble, they will still be 'on your side'.

9. Be prepared
Practise, but don't try to memorize every detail and every word you want to say. It helps to have general notes for your presentation in the sequence you want to discuss things. It can be very stressful if you feel you need to recite a short essay. Practise with friends or colleagues so that they can give you feedback.

10. Content is king
Content is paramount. Always try to ensure the content is actually worth presenting and make sure the presentation is visually stimulating. It's easier to present if the audience is looking at the slides or pages and not at you all the time, so give them something good to look at.

Fig. 2
(Opposite) An informal presentation taking place at the Seren design studio in London. Seren employs a diverse range of creative employees from different disciplines such as product design, interaction design, sociology and computing science.

Report creation

By documenting your decision-making process, you will enable the creation of a readily understood archive of the rationale behind your design decisions. Such a report is useful for assimilating new team members and for quickly assessing the impact of changes as the product moves through design process towards manufacture and its launch in the marketplace.

Report writing in design is becoming increasingly commonplace in contemporary design projects and is an important skill for designers to acquire. Writing good design reports can be a real challenge, as they often need to reflect the final results of complex projects that have included detailed research, sometimes undertaken over a significant period of time. Usually, however, a lot of the detail must be left out of the main part of the report; instead the report should focus on the presentation of summary information, including the rationale behind critical design decisions leading to your overall recommendations. The detail can be placed in the appendices instead, and accessed later if needed.

A design report must comprise the following main levels of information:
— Executive summary
— Introduction
— Analysis
— Conclusion
— Appendices

The report should be well structured, stating your outcomes and recommendations clearly, using well-designed diagrams, charts and images, and providing the reader with a concise summary of the research conducted. A key element in a good design report is a clear structure. The following structural guidelines will help you create excellent reports every time.

1. Title page – this provides the title of the project, client name, date, your name and your organization.

2. Summary – this sets the problem in context, summarizes what you have done, and lists the key outcomes and recommendations.

3. Table of contents – this page clearly outlines each part of the report using section headings and page numbers.

4. Introduction – this both introduces and situates the problem being addressed, and discusses any previous research in the area.

5. Analysis section(s) (usually given specific titles) – this provides a walkthrough of the analyses that led to your overall recommendations. You should keep this simple throughout, using only essential diagrams, charts and images. Remember that the detail (e.g. raw data) should be placed in the appendices.

6. Conclusion – this should give a brief summary of what you have done, and include your recommendations.

7. References – this is a list in standard form of all the books, journals, magazines, scientific reports, websites and other resources you have referred to in the report.

8. Bibliography – this contains other books and resources you used during the study that might not be referenced explicitly in the report.

9. Appendices – you may have more than one appendix, which will describe in detail, if necessary, the analyses you have undertaken for the brief and the data you have obtained.

After you have written your design report, it is a good idea to go through the following questions to ensure you have covered everything:

— Have you answered the brief?
— Have you clearly understood the context of the problem?
— Have you fully articulated the analyses you have undertaken in the project?
— Have you clearly illustrated your results in diagrams, charts and images?
— Have you written the executive summary in clear and concise terms?
— Have you used appropriate and relevant vocabulary?
— Does the layout of your report clearly map the progression of your design project, including your research and results?

Fig. 3
Representative pages from a student report exploring how waste from the food industry can be utilized.

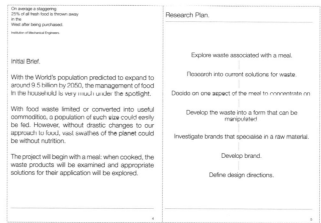

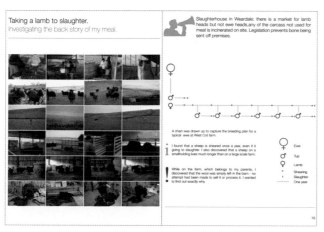

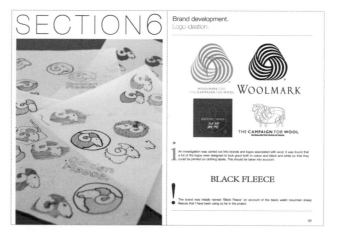

Presentation visuals and models

During the development of a new product, a product designer will often make hundreds of quick sketches and models. However, when presenting these ideas to the client and others in order to communicate intentions of size, shape, scale and materials, these rough sketches and models will need to be tidied up so as to present something more visually seductive.

The designer has to shift from a three-dimensional idea into a two-dimensional sketch, and then back again into a three-dimensional representation of that idea. The widespread adoption of CAD has led to many designers developing their ideas virtually, visualizing their new products and concepts through photorealistic renderings of 3D models and scenes. The use of digital models allows for the quick exploration of new design ideas, materials and textures, and often provides a more cost-effective alternative when it comes to producing physical presentation models and photographing them.

However, while digital models are ideal for generating visuals for marketing and advertising material and presentations of new products, there is no substitute for a well-resolved tangible physical model that consumers and clients can see, feel and engage with. Product design is a three-dimensional discipline, and while the immediacy of marker renderings and the visual gloss and ease of CAD offer huge possibilities, it is essential that designers model their concepts physically and test and present them in the real world.

Presentation guidelines

When visualizing, modelling and presenting design concepts you should adhere to the following points:

— Visualize early – Don't just visualize as a presentation tool, but as a concept generation device that can convey your concepts clearly and concisely to as wide an audience as possible.
— Iterate often – Iterate as much as possible during the initial stages of the design process. This will help you generate ideas in a manner more conducive to evaluating a concept's merits rather than falling for the superficial qualities of a particular visual.
— Don't over-visualize – The aim of concept generation is to generate as many viable concepts as possible. Low-fidelity, rapid sketches and models are far more useful at this stage of the design process than more polished techniques, as they encourage debate.
— Visualize neutrally – When evaluating alternate design options it really helps to keep the quality and style of each visual or model as similar as possible. By presenting designs in a neutral manner, you can shed a sense of ownership, and the efforts of the entire team can be evaluated on a level playing field.
— Be aware of how people interpret visuals – You need to be fully aware of the subtle messages that different forms of visuals carry. For example, a rough pencil sketch has an immediacy that might imply an underdeveloped concept, while a photorealistic computer rendering may imply that what is, in fact, a mere concept, is a finished design that is beyond criticism or change.

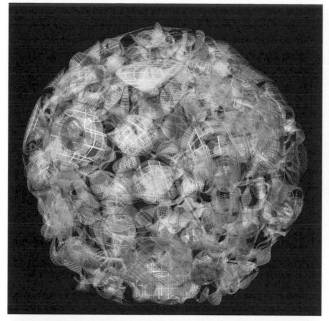

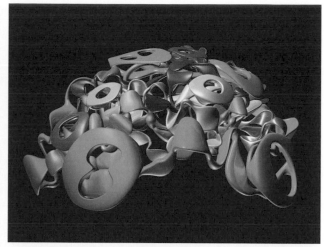

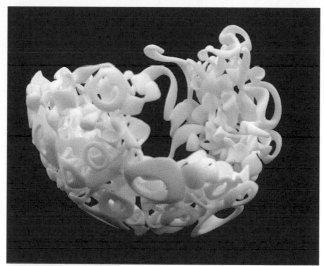

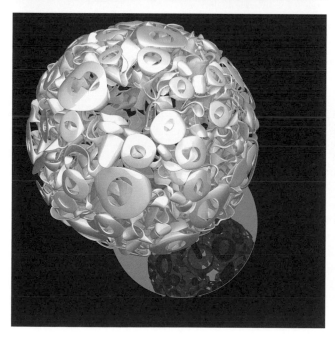

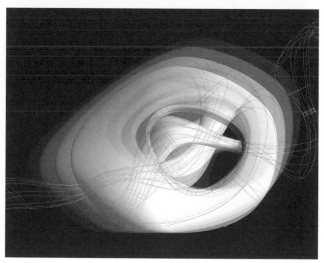

Fig. 4
Presentation visuals used to demonstrate the digital manufacture of the Entropia Light by Lionel T. Dean.

Engaging the public

Design research cannot reside in an academic ivory tower or insular design studio, and academic and professional design researchers are increasingly seeking to engage the public in their research activities, and to share the benefits with the public. Engagement is by definition a two-way process, involving dialogue and interaction with stakeholders, with the goal of generating mutually beneficial outcomes.

Public engagement can dramatically improve the quality and relevance of your research, helping you to refine your ideas and develop your presentation and communication skills. Those who engage with your research can play an invaluable role in contributing to that research, while stimulating their curiosity for your work and the products you are developing. Not only do the public raise relevant questions but projects that have been defined and researched in partnership with the public also often result in greater disciplinary and commercial impact and relevance.

Public engagement covers a range of different activities, from traditional one-way forms of engagement such as public lectures and talks, to more interactive forms of engagement such as participatory design. As a design researcher it is all too easy to lose perspective on why your research matters, especially when addressing longer-term speculative research that may only be commercialized in years to come. Discussing your work with the public can help you question your assumptions, introduce fresh perspectives to improve your thinking, and provide an opportunity to reflect on your design practice and research.

When determining how to present your research and engage the public, you need to consider the following:

Purpose
You should think about why you want to engage the public with your research. This can be challenging but it's often hard to determine a clear public engagement approach without knowing why you are doing it in the first place. Are you seeking to disseminate the results of your research? Are you hoping to encourage people to help you develop your design research further? Are you trying to promote your approach to design and the creative methods you employ? Are you aiming to consult the public on their views of your design research?

Audience
You need to think about who you are hoping to engage with. Who are your audience? How can you ensure you engage with them effectively? It is easy to think that your audience is an all-inclusive notion of the 'general public', but who are the key stakeholders in your design research? Once you have identified your audience, you should focus on understanding their interests and lifestyles. Why might they be interested in taking part in your public engagement activity? The more you understand your audience, the more successful your public engagement activity is likely to be.

Activity
You need to determine what you are trying to do through engaging with the public. You need to be realistic about the resources you have at your disposal, and ensure you are fully prepared to run the activity in an appropriate manner. There are lots of ways of engaging with the public, and you can present your work to audiences through a variety of forms, such as exhibitions, presentations, workshops, lectures, talks, blogs, forums and press activities.

Assessment

Once you have undertaken the activity, you need to evaluate what you have learnt from the process. You should ensure that the aims of your public engagement are achievable, and make your objectives SMART: Specific, Measurable, Achievable, Relevant and Time-limited. You can undertake ongoing evaluation (formative) to assess how successful your event is in engaging with your audience. This allows you to modify what you are doing. Finally, you can conduct summative evaluation at the end of the event to assess the success in achieving your outputs (results of your activity), outcomes (overall benefits) and the overall impact (effect and influence of the activity).

Communication skills are at the heart of public engagement, so you should adhere to the following guidelines:

- Adapt your presentation approach and content for different audiences.

- Listen to your audience and respond carefully to their questions and inputs.

- Respect and value your audience's contributions.

- Build on your audience's knowledge and understanding.

- Welcome feedback.

- Reflect on your own practice.

- Conduct formative and summative evaluation.

- Recognize when to seek advice or support from colleagues, key audience members and presentation experts.

- Be sensitive to issues of diversity and inclusion.

- Respect differences in understanding and attitudes.

- Be alert to social and ethical issues.

- Build and sustain effective partnerships.

Case Study

AMO / Rem Koolhaas Roadmap 2050 project

Introduction

The work of Rem Koolhaas and OMA has won several international awards, including the Pritzker Architecture Prize in 2000, the RIBA Gold Medal (UK) in 2004 and the Mies van der Rohe European Union Prize for Contemporary Architecture in 2005. OMA's recent projects include the new headquarters for China Central and the Shenzhen Stock Exchange in China, De Rotterdam (the largest building in the Netherlands), the Zeche Zollverein historical museum in Germany, the Seoul National University Museum of Art and the much acclaimed Casa da Música in Portugal. The counterpart to OMA's architectural practice is AMO, a design and research think tank based in Rotterdam.

Objective

While OMA remains dedicated to the realization of buildings, AMO operates in areas beyond the traditional boundaries of architecture, including product design, media, politics, sociology, renewable energy, technology, fashion, curating, publishing and graphic design. AMO often works in parallel with OMA's clients to fertilize architecture with intelligence gleaned from this array of disciplines.

AMO has been involved in a number of high-profile renewable energy projects, including Zeekracht for the North Sea and The Energy Report for the World Wildlife Fund. In October 2009, European leaders committed to an 80 to 95 per cent reduction in CO2 emissions by 2050. Roadmap 2050 was commissioned to determine how this goal could efficiently be met.

Methods

In design, the issue of sustainability is generally dealt with at the scale of products or buildings. Roadmap 2050 adopts a fundamentally different approach, seeking solutions that transcend the scale of a building, a city or even a nation. AMO developed a vision for an EU-wide de-carbonized power grid by 2050 through the creation of a report, proposing a practical guide to a prosperous, low-carbon Europe.

Results

The technical and economic analyses of the Roadmap 2050 report outline why a zero-carbon power sector is required to meet this commitment and illustrate its feasibility by 2050 given current technology. AMO contributed to the content development through the production of a graphic narrative about the geographical, political and cultural implications of a zero-carbon power sector. This narrative shows how through the complete integration and synchronization of the EU's energy infrastructure, Europe can take maximum advantage of its geographical diversity. If the Roadmap is followed, by 2050, the simultaneous presence of various renewable energy sources within the EU will create a complementary system of energy provision, ensuring energy security for future generations. Roadmap 2050 was commissioned by the European Climate Foundation, and the full report includes extensive technical, economic and policy analyses.

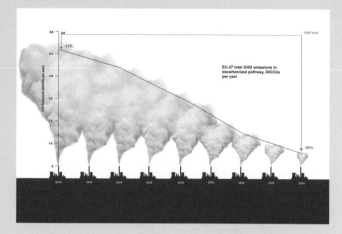

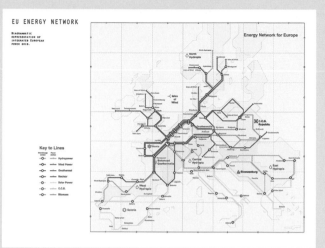

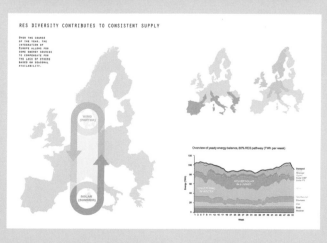

Conveying complex concepts is a key skill required by the contemporary designer. AMO adopted a diverse range of approaches to communicate their research findings for the Roadmap 2050 research project, from photo collage to information graphics, schematic diagrams and provocative renderings.

Case Study

Konstantin Grcic
Serpentine Gallery

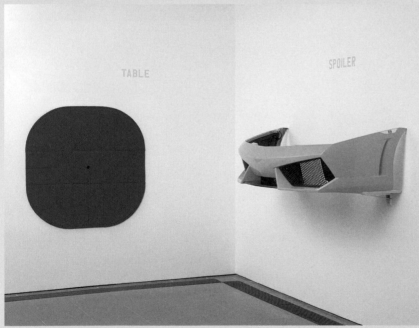

The Design Real exhibition featured everyday designed components and products such as a polycarbonate Volvo car Tail light, Herman Miller Aeron Office Chair and birch wood child's toy bike by Kokua Holzspielzeug GmbH.

Introduction

The Serpentine Gallery is one of London's best-loved galleries for modern and contemporary art, and its exhibition, architecture and educational programmes attract up to 800,000 visitors a year. In 2009–10 the gallery held its first design-focused show, entitled 'Design Real', curated by one of the world's leading industrial designers, Konstantin Grcic, and designed in collaboration with Alex Rich and Jürg Lehni. Grcic is dedicated to the importance of good design in everyday life and this ethos was at the very core of the exhibition.

Objective

In the words of Konstantin Grcic, 'Good design admits to the deeper insight that beyond performing a purpose in a good way, the purpose itself has to be good. All 43 items in the exhibition fulfil this idea in their own way. The relevance a product has to our life lies not only in its use, but also in how far we identify with it. A good product becomes part of our culture'.

Methods

Art galleries have traditionally adopted a questionable approach to displaying design, focusing on pure aesthetics and exclusively crafted historic products, while promoting leading designers as individual artists, divorced from the realities of the design manufacturing and development process. Indeed, one could argue that the only difference between an institution such as the Terence Conran-endorsed Design Museum in London, and his Conran Shop design emporium, is that the designer chairs and knick-knacks you can buy in the shop are placed on pedestals or within glass vitrines in the gallery.

ARMOUR

The 'Design Real' exhibition broke radically with this and adopted a new approach to public engagement, displaying a selection of 'real', mass-produced items that had a practical function in everyday life. There were no prototypes, concepts or models featured; all of the products were in serial production and were more or less available for individuals to buy. Moreover, all of the objects on display had been conceived within the previous ten years.

Results

Grcic brought together a wide range of products with different styles and functions, from furniture and household items to technical and industrial innovations. In the galleries, the items were identified by broad, generic categories. Additional contextual information was omitted in order to encourage an unmediated encounter with the exhibits on display. In the Serpentine's large central room, Grcic designed a research space for visitors to further investigate these objects, and access the exhibition's accompanying website and central research resource. The website was a parallel reality, a database that investigated the products in detail, exploring aspects of their development, production and use. 'Design Real' enabled visitors to ponder the relationship between beauty and function, and demonstrated a valuable new approach to exhibiting design products and the processes behind their creation, consumption and use.

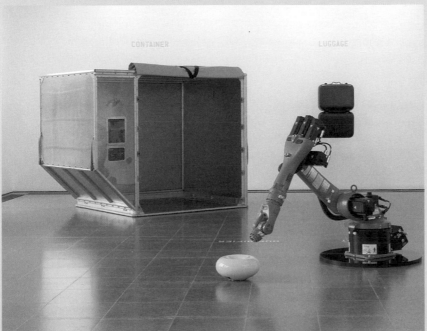

Above: Products were deliberately placed out of context and in unusual juxtapositions.

Below: Products on display included a PalNet aluminium container and a Kuka Automation robot arm.

How to create a great research presentation

When presenting your research it is essential to show the entire process from initial sketches such as those above, through to the final resolved research findings.

Before you begin, think carefully about what you need to include in your presentation. If necessary, you might wish to clarify with your clients, collaborators and stakeholders exactly what is required of you and what facilities you can utilize. In terms of the visual aspects of your presentation, use magazines, books, publications and other materials as a source for your layout designs. The following guidelines provide a number of suggestions on how to maximize the impact of your presentation and your presentation skills:

White space

Don't overload the page with too many visuals or text; the most effective layouts are simple and allow some white space. Background colours on sheets are often difficult to handle and can easily make your work look less professional. White always works well.

Hierarchy

Make sure there is a variety of image and text sizes so that the important aspects stand out. Your key image should be noticeably larger than others so that it's the first thing a viewer looks at on the page. By making sure there is a hierarchy of information, you can control how a viewer reads the page.

Scale

When creating a hierarchy of information and imagery, consider using a set number of sizes for images and text throughout the entire presentation. This gives consistency and helps create a look for all the pages. It also makes it much faster to put a presentation together. For example, all title text in Arial 20 point bold, all descriptive text in Arial 12

point regular, and all caption text in Arial 9 point bold and italic. The same rules can be applied to the images, by making sure, for example, that all key images and smaller images are consistently sized.

Text

Choose one font for the entire presentation but use different styles and sizes to indicate the hierarchy for titles, descriptive text and captions. A sans-serif font is one that has no flicks on the letters; these are often clean, modern and understated. Good sans-serif fonts are Helvetica, Gill Sans, Futura and Arial.

A serif font has flicks on the letters; they are often classic, book-like and traditional. Good serif fonts are Times New Roman, Baskerville, Garamond and Palatino. There is a huge variety of fonts available, and this is very much a personal choice, but the ones above are a good starting point.

Never use white text on a black background, as it is difficult to read, particularly a serif font in a small size. Never have a line length of more than 12 to 15 words – people will forget the last word of a line by the time their eye moves to the start of the next line, and so won't be able to absorb the information properly.

Format

Choose a format – landscape or portrait – that suits your project and use it consistently for all the pages in your presentation.

Printing

If you are using hand-made elements or drawings, scan them and insert them digitally onto the page. Do not glue them onto the final sheet.

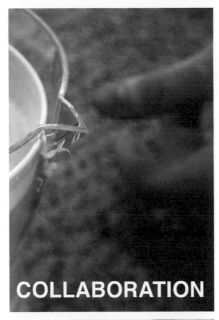

COLLABORATION

Collaborators

Therefore

Dan Kayser
Julia Allwright
Mario Siquiera

The three named above all work for Therefore Product Design Consultancy. Each one specialising in certain areas, Julia being engineer based, Dan a design engineer and Mario focusing on interaction.

I completed my placement at Therefore and find it very easy to speak to their people to get feedback. I keep in touch on a regular basis and the company as a whole seem more than happy to help me out. Including the use of their workshop, which could prove invaluable.

Designers & Artists

Alkesh Parmer

A recent graduate from the RCA, Alkesh completed a project were he successfully re used the rind from hesperidin fruits to transform it into a sustainable material and or products. He created an orange juicer from waste orange peel.

Terry Stokes

A personal acquaintance from placement. Terry is currently freelancing but was very willing and helpful when feedback was required.

It is great to have someone on board who has a bit of experience in the area of orange juicing, such as Alkesh. He is keen for me to show off my knowledge about oranges and the research that was done.

Terry is a personal friend I met on placement and is more than happy to give frank and honest feedback on a regular basis. On both design and engineering aspects.

Orange Expert

Rupen Parmer

Rupen is a bit of an expert when it comes to juicing and the business surrounding it. He set up his business, 'Bjuiced' where he owns juice bars and off site catering - "street juice". Also running a juicing consultancy and retreats.

It would have been remiss of me to not have advice from someone who knows the juicing business inside out. Although Rupen is a busy man we usually speak on the phone every other week. His insight into the business aspect of this market has made quite an impact on the decision making process of my project. Pushing me away from designing for the street and more for a cafe culture.

collaborators   24

Images

Source material from the internet carefully. There is nothing worse than a small pixelated image in a presentation.

Printing

Always allow time to print a black and white version of the presentation pages to check how things look. Often what you see on the screen looks very different from what will be printed on a sheet of paper, particularly the scale of text and images. Also print out a test of any colour images to check that they are true to the tones you've chosen on-screen.

Editing

Often you will have to be selective about what you show in a presentation; not everything needs to be used, and not all text is necessary for people to understand the concept or work. Allow time to put the presentation together, to print it and then look at how much you are trying to include; have a colleague look at it with you and discuss whether you need less or more to communicate your ideas.

Size

As a rule, illustrations, sketches, collages and so on look better slightly smaller on the page. Reducing their size can often make them look more intricate and seductive.

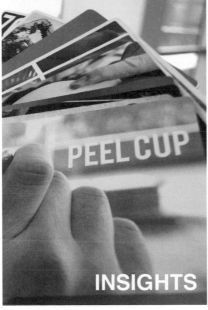

PEEL CUP

INSIGHTS

Exploration Cards

A pack of cards were submitted as part of a hand in for the exploration cards. The idea behind the cards was that one could be picked at random and it would provide an insight into the project.

The following pages contain a selection of these cards.

TEAPOT POUR

The amount of pouring the juicer like a teapot was unconscious and lead to more thought around the idea of ritual.

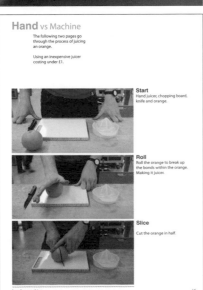

Hand vs Machine

The following two pages go through the process of juicing an orange.

Using an inexpensive juicer costing under £1.

Start
Hand juicer, chopping board, knife and orange.

Roll
Roll the orange to break up the bonds within the orange. Making it juicer.

Slice
Cut the orange in half.

hand vs machine   16

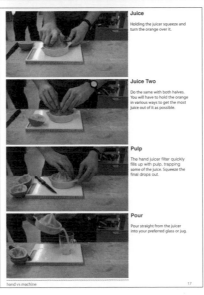

Juice
Holding the juicer squeeze and turn the orange over it.

Juice Two
Do the same with both halves. You will have to hold the orange in various ways to get the most juice out of it as possible.

Pulp
The hand juicer filter quickly fills up with pulp, trapping some of the juice. Squeeze the final drops out.

Pour
Pour straight from the juicer into your preferred glass or jug.

hand vs machine   17

Sample pages from a student report. A step-by-step approach ensures that the depth and breadth of research can be appreciated, evaluated and approved.

Tutorial

How to create a great research report

Creating a successful research report requires thought and time.

A research report is an account of the observations or study conducted by the report writer (researcher). A report can be written by almost anybody who can present his or her record of observations. However, there are several factors that will differentiate a good report from a bad one. Reports are only good if they reflect an accurate or faithful recollection of the events conducted, including the observation of people, products and processes, or information obtained from reading and/or past records. Bad and/or wrong data, such as manipulated or manufactured data, will result in a bad report.

Objectivity is another important characteristic in the quality of a report. A report must be an accurate account of the original information gathered; you must present the plain facts as you discovered them. Reporting, intentional or otherwise, that alters or modifies the nature of these facts would constitute bias or subjectivity and every effort must be made to produce an unbiased presentation.

A clear and well-organized format is a primary requirement of a good report. Often the specifications of the report will be stated by the recipient (e.g. the client, stakeholder, collaborator). However, as a general rule, nearly all forms of formal communication have the following main components.

Beginning (brief introduction)

First, introduce your study. State the origin and the rationale behind the idea (background). Support your rationale with previous studies, listing only the most significant and relevant sources (literature review). State clearly the main issues related to your study. These will form the focus of your report (objectives). State the benefits, relevance and advantages that will result from your study findings (significance of the study). Report how you conducted your study and describe your methodological strategy in tackling the issues (methodology) and the data collection procedures and instruments you used. For example, if you conducted a plain literature survey, include your plan and procedures for this with your gathered materials.

Middle (main section)

This section is the heart of your report and should contain all the main findings of your study (results). You should group similar findings under subheadings and support your statements with relevant previous studies or well-known facts and opinions. Remember, you are reporting the state of knowledge surrounding your study problem and you need to be accurate with every account. Be objective in your entire presentation of the results. Just present the facts that you have found, and leave the readers of your report some room for individual interpretation and judgement.

In subsequent sub-sections, present your own analyses, opinions and criticisms, supported by relevant literature and previous studies. You may like to title the heading of this section something like 'Results and discussions'.

End (concluding section)

Sum up the most important findings and insights in your report (summary) and reflect on whether you addressed all of the objectives in your study or not, stating briefly the limitations of your study. Finish your report with recommendations that leave readers with precise answers to your questions. Also, list any implications and applications of the study, and suggest where a subsequent researcher(s) might go from here. This should include a section where you cite formally all your sources of information (references) so that readers of the report have the opportunity to verify or redo your study. Finally, you may have to include an section where you can attach any additional information or relevant materials – such as tables, graphs, photos or CDs – that you have used in the report (appendices).

These representative pages demonstrate the range of approaches and depth required for a typical research report. A coherent graphical style ensures that the reader can focus on the content.

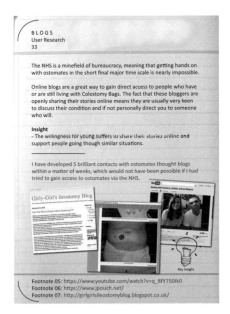

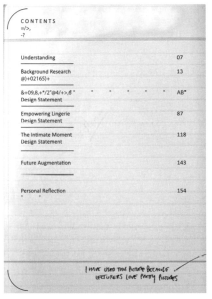

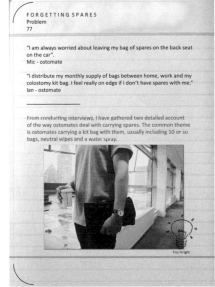

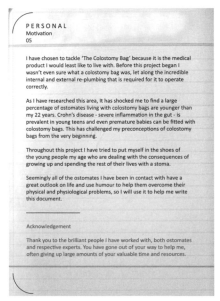

RESEARCH METHODS
FOR PRODUCT DESIGN

SUMMARY

GLOSSARY

RESOURCES

INDEX

PICTURE CREDITS

ACKNOWLEDGMENTS

SUMMARY

This book has introduced a rich and diverse range of research methods and tools, along with ideas of how and when to deploy these methods effectively – all of which can be used to inform your design thinking and doing.

Each method will contribute a firm foundation for your design research, while the tutorials and real-world examples provided in the case studies will encourage you to develop your own research approach and toolkit. Here is a summary of the key points of the book, and of product design.

Looking

Design research usually starts with looking – observing the world around you, and using research methods to discover what people really need, want and do rather than just what they say they need, want and do. Observing and examining peoples' emotional attachments to their belongings, and carrying out the forensic analysis of designed products with a critical eye, can also help you to design and develop better products.

Learning

Designers can then learn from what people really need, want and do by using effective techniques such as precedent analysis, role playing and 'try it yourself'. Adopting these methods will enable you to learn first-hand what using a particular product in a specific context feels like.

Asking

A variety of straightforward ways of obtaining information from users, such as questionnaires, focus groups, interviews and the creation of personas, will rapidly provide you with an understanding of the multifaceted relationships that exists between users and the designed products and services they use every day.

Making

You can then move into the creation of models and prototypes to help inform your design and decision-making processes, communicate your design concepts, and enable users and clients to understand and explore how they might like to engage with the planned product or service.

Testing

A range of testing methods, including user trials, test rigs and safety testing, will then aid informed decision-making, and ensure a streamlined design and development process that avoids costly mistakes or delays.

Selection & Evaluation

Selecting the wrong product design proposal to develop can be very costly to manufacturers and stakeholders in terms of time, money and other valuable resources – the numerous systematic methods for evaluating and selecting design proposals described will help maximize your chances of selecting the right one.

Communicating

The final stage of the design research process is communication. It is essential for a designer to be able to communicate clearly with potential customers, clients and stakeholders. Ideas and thoughts can be disseminated to the various people involved in a design project through the use of design sketches, prototypes, presentation models and other more formal presentations. Good communication is key to successfully presenting product design research and practice. By using a number of the established and emergent research methods contained within this book, you can help ensure you develop your designs in a carefully considered, transparent, iterative process.

Conclusions

Design research employs both qualitative and quantitative research methods, including ethnography, mapping, trend forecasting, cultural comparisons, video diaries, probes and a host of other methods, to help shape our global future. Design projects now routinely transcend economic, national and cultural borders, and this increasingly challenging environment requires that product designers understand different cultures, evaluate design proposals sensitively and communicate with people from very different backgrounds.

New digital information and communication technologies provide amazing means of communicating, learning and making, but these can also make a designer's life more complicated. In addition, environmental concerns are now so grave that a rise in global temperatures above two degrees Celsius could be catastrophic.

The implications for product designers today, therefore, run to some very serious social, cultural and environmental issues. It is hoped that this book will inspire you to research and develop future products that are sensitive to these issues, and to help shape a future world worth living in.

Glossary

appearance model
A model created to simulate the look and physical characteristics, rather than the function, of a proposed product.

bodystorming
A research method in which a design team attempts to physically recreate a situation through role-play, in order to better imagine its social and physical considerations.

boundary user
A user on the limit of being able to use a product, a useful consideration in identifying opportunities for design improvement.

brand DNA analysis
Multilayered analysis of a branded product, integrating quantitative data and qualitative research from many sources.

brandscaping
A structured evaluation of an industry sector achieved by selecting the products most representative of each brand, and comparing their most characteristic elements and important features.

CAD
Computer-aided design, also computer-aided drafting. The use of computer systems to assist in the creation, modification, analysis or optimization of a design.

clay model
A product model literally made of clay or industrial plasticine; also a generic term for **appearance models** of any material, as these were frequently made of clay in the past.

competitor product analysis
Examining and evaluating a product and its competitors with respect to a predefined set of both qualitative and quantitative criteria.

concept map
A graphic illustration in which two or more concepts are linked by words that describe their relationship. Developed by Professor Joseph D. Novak at Cornell University in the 1960s.

crowdsourcing
Outsourcing tasks traditionally performed by experts to a group of people through an online open call.

crowdvoting
A form of **crowdsourcing** that makes use of the power of popular opinion and doubles as a marketing tool: companies ask users to vote ideas up or down in real time, simultaneously generating useful feedback and consumer interest.

cultural comparisons
The careful use of personal or published accounts to reveal differences in national or cultural behavioural traits, which will have design implications when producing for global markets.

cultural probe
A means of gathering information in a creative manner with minimal intrusion: subjects are provided with items such as cameras, voice recorders and notebooks, and asked to record and report back on their experiences over a period of time.

a day in the life
An intensive research method that aims to provide a representative snapshot of the life of a potential product user, and may reveal issues inherent in their routines and circumstances.

digital ethnography
The use of digital tools such as cameras, computers and the internet to accelerate the process of data collection, analysis and presentation in **ethnography**.

drop testing
Measuring the durability of a part or material by subjecting it to a free fall from a predetermined height on to a surface, under prescribed conditions.

empathy tools
Physical or software devices that designers can use to reduce their ability to interact with a product, and thereby gain an impression of the experiences of users with disabilities or special conditions. Also known as 'capability simulators'.

end-user
The person who ultimately uses a product, as opposed to others who may handle it or purchase it within a supply chain.

ethnography
The study of the culture, knowledge, language, values and system of meanings of a people or group.

experience prototyping
Any kind of non-physical representation of a product, which itself might be a service, lifestyle or experience, that enables a design team to learn from a simulation of the proposed product's use in different contexts.

extreme user
An individual who is either extremely familiar or completely unfamiliar with a particular product, service or system.

failure modes and effects analysis (FMEA)
A structured risk analysis tool to identify, quantify and mitigate the specific risks associated with individual assemblies or components by determining the location and nature of a failure.

focus group
A number of people brought together in one place to discuss a particular issue or set of issues, such as their experiences of a particular product, service or system.

future forecasting
The identification of future aesthetic

preferences as well as the prediction of global ecological, technological and financial changes, to help designers anticipate future needs.

image board *see* **mood board**

inclusive design
The design of mainstream products and services that are accessible to, and usable by, as many people as reasonably possible without the need for special adaptation or specialized design.

literature review
A text considering the critical points of current knowledge on a topic, including substantive findings as well as the theoretical and methodological. A detailed form of **secondary research**.

market positioning
The decisions made by an organization about how they want users to see their product relative to the existing market or **brandscape**.

matrix evaluation
A quantitative technique used to evaluate concept design proposals by ranking them against set criteria stated in the **product design specification (PDS)** or other concept design proposals. Sometimes referred to as 'Pugh's Method' after its creator, Professor Stuart Pugh.

metrics
The set of qualitative features chosen by researchers to be measured in product usability tests.

mind map
A visual representation of hierarchical information, made popular by the psychologist Tony Buzan, and intended to represent words and ideas in a way that engages both sides of the brain.

mock-up
An easily fabricated, life-size physical model constructed from rough materials, used to evaluate the physical interaction, scale and proportion of product design concepts.

mood board
A collaged board containing images, text and samples of objects, used by designers to portray a range of potential directions for a specific product or brand, to help develop and communicate design concepts. Also known as an 'image board'.

mystery shopper
A researcher posing as a regular consumer, whose job it is to carry out market research or internal quality control with their identity concealed.

name swapping
A market research technique, which involves swapping the names and logos on different product designs from the same market, and discussing if and why the resulting designs are 'wrong' for the branded products being researched.

pen portrait *see* **persona**

perceptual mapping
Arranging market research data on an X–Y axis to visually compare attributes such as the perceived cost, quality and impact of a brand or product. Used to evaluate corporate design positioning strategy.

persona
A fictional character, based on real-life observations of archetypal users, created to represent groups of users within a targeted demographic who might all use particular products, brands and services in a similar way. Also known as a 'pen portrait'.

primary research
Original research undertaken by the design researcher. More time-consuming and costly than **secondary research**.

product autopsy
The analysis of a product that has reached the end of its life, often involving a full disassembly, to discover how each component has fared, as well as to assess the design in more general terms.

product camouflage
A research method involving the modification of a series of existing designs, each with different elements removed. Through **focus group** discussions, the value of each element can be determined.

product champion
A member of the new-product design and development team who supports the instigation and development of concept design and acts as a go-between linking various departments within an organization, becoming an expert on that particular product.

product collage
A **mood board** created by potential users as part of design research, to help them articulate complex ideas and perceptions related to a design issue.

product design specification (PDS)
A document that clearly sets out the parameters that must be met by a design, presented initially before a project is taken on, but often adapted throughout the design process.

proof of concept model
Mock-ups that do not incorporate any product styling and are only intended to demonstrate the basic mechanism of a product, as proof of its potential viability.

Pugh's Method *see* **matrix evaluation**

qualitative research
Research into consumer or user behaviour that focuses on questions of *why* and *how* decisions or actions are made, often using smaller but more focused sample groups.

quantitative research
Research into consumer or user behaviour focusing on objective questions of *what*, *where* and *when* decisions or actions are made, ideally using large sample groups and producing results that can be displayed as graphs or statistics.

quick-and-dirty prototype
Quickly built prototypes using rough materials for speed, which are used to communicate a concept to other members of a design team. Also known as 'rough-and-ready prototype'.

rapid ethnography
An approximate form of **ethnography**, used when quick results are required.

rapid iterative testing and evaluation (RITE)
A form of product usability testing that encourages testers to 'think aloud' (**user narration**), enabling the designer to step in and change the user interface of a product the moment a problem has been identified and a rapid solution has been devised.

rapid prototyping
The automatic construction of detailed physical objects from computer data using a range of 3D printing technologies.

role playing
A process in which designers assume the role of the various stakeholders in a project and act out scenarios to gain a better understanding of important issues.

rough-and-ready prototype *see* **quick-and-dirty prototype**

sampling
Selecting a subset of individuals, objects or items for study, intended to be representative of the wider group, from a population or marketplace.

scenario testing
The creation of future scenarios, demonstrating speculative products being used by ordinary people in realistic future contexts, presented through storyboards, texts, photography, film and plays, which can help product designers communicate and evaluate design proposals within their intended context.

schematic sketches
Sketches describing the fixed dimensional parameters of a design, including vital data such as off-the-shelf components to be used and ergonomic considerations, with less emphasis on appearance.

secondary research
The summary, collation and/or synthesis of existing research.

semiotics
The study of the use and understanding of signs within a particular culture.

shadowing
A method in which a researcher closely follows an individual or small team over an extended period of time throughout their working day.

sketch model
Generally crude full-size or scale models that aim to capture the embryonic ideas emerging from the design team's initial concept development; often an early attempt to realize a design in three dimensions before proceeding with more detailed work.

stereolithography
An additive manufacturing process used in 3D printing, which builds up layers of solid plastic using an ultraviolet laser and a liquid resin vat. Used for **rapid prototyping**.

test rig
A **mock-up** that replicates a mechanical action or enables a physical property of a design, such as its strength, stiffness, comfort or durability, to be tested.

thematic sketches
Intentionally fluid, dynamic and expressive exploratory sketches, which convey a product's physical form, characteristics and overall aesthetic.

think aloud protocols *see* **user narration**

touchpoint
The means by which a user comes into contact with a product throughout its lifecycle, including interactive internet features, printed documents, physical devices, retail outlets and call centres.

touchpoint wheel
A tool for analyzing the entire customer journey, which summarizes all the points of interaction where a customer can be intentionally or unintentionally influenced.

trend forecaster
A specialist working within a market research or similar organization who postulates possible future trends in fashion, culture and technology by evaluating past and present trends.

trend spotting
Detailed analysis of new design, commercial, visual or fashion trends as they begin to appear, looking at their qualities and probable development.

try it yourself
The act of using a prototype, existing or new product as part of the research process in order to gain first-hand experience of how it performs and how it feels to use it.

type testing
Benchmark tests, particular to a specific type of product, normally laid out by an independent quality-control organization in order to provide fair and balanced comparison.

unfocus group
A method for gaining a number of interpretations on a given design problem employing diverse individuals in a workshop-style setting

contributing to concept design
generation or evaluation activities.

user narration
A method for identifying users'
concerns when using specific
products, systems and services by
asking them to think about and
describe aloud their experience as
they engage with or use them.
Sometimes referred to as 'think aloud
protocols'.

user trials
Trials of either new or existing
products carried out by groups of
users under controlled conditions.
These often use prototypes as a
cheaper alternative to field trials with a
finished product.

Resources

Further reading

Albrecht, D. et al, *Design Culture Now*, Laurence King Publishing, London, 2000

Antonelli, P., *Humble Masterpieces: 100 Everyday Marvels of Design*, Thames & Hudson, London, 2006

Antonelli, P., *Supernatural: The Work of Ross Lovegrove*, Phaidon Press, London, 2004

Antonelli, P. and Aldersey-Williams, H., *Design and the Elastic Mind*, The Museum of Modern Art, New York, 2008

Arad, R. et al, *Spoon*, Phaidon Press, London, 2002

Asensio, P., *Product Design*, teNeues Publishing Group, New York, 2002

Baxter, M., *Product Design*, Chapman Hall, London, 1995

Bohm, F., *KGID: Konstantin Grcic Industrial Design*, Phaidon Press, London, 2007

Bone, M. and Johnson, K., *I Miss My Pencil*, Chronicle Books, San Francisco, 2009

Bouroullec, R. and Bouroullec, E., *Ronan and Erwan Bouroullec*, Phaidon Press, London, 2003

Bramston, D., *Basics Product Design: Idea Searching*, AVA Publishing, Lausanne, 2008

Bramston, D., *Basics Product Design: Material Thoughts*, AVA Publishing, Lausanne, 2009

Bramston, D., *Basics Product Design: Visual Conversations: 3*, AVA Publishing, Lausanne, 2009

Brown, T., *Change by Design: How Design Thinking Creates New Alternatives for Business and Society: How Design Thinking Can Transform Organizations and Inspire Innovation*, Collins Business, London, 2009

Bryman, A., *Social Research Methods*, Oxford University Press, Oxford, 2001

Burroughs, A., *Everyday Engineering*, Chronicle Books, San Francisco, 2007

Busch, A., *Design is…Words, Things, People, Buildings and Places*, Metropolis Books, Princeton Architectural Press, 2002

Byars, M., *The Design Encyclopaedia*, John Wiley & Sons, New York, 1994

Campos, C., *Product Design Now*, Harper Design International, London, 2006

Castelli, C.T., *Transitive Design*, Edizioni Electa, Milan, 2000

Chia, Patrick, *Design Incubator: a Prototype for New Design Practice*, Laurence King Publishers, London, 2013

Chua, C.K., *Rapid Prototyping*, World Scientific, London, 2003

Cooper, R. and Press, M., *Design Management: Managing Design*, John Wiley & Sons, London, 1995

Crouch, C. and Pearce, J. *Doing Research in Design*, Berg, Oxford, 2012

Cross, N., *Engineering Design Methods*, John Wiley & Sons, Chichester, 1989

Curedale, R., *Design Research Methods: 150 ways to inform design*, Design Community College Inc., Los Angeles, 2013

Dixon, T. et al, *And Fork: 100 Designers, 10 Curators, 10 Good Designs*, Phaidon Press, London, 2007

Dormer, P., *Design since 1945*, Thames & Hudson, London, 1993

Dormer, P., *The Meanings of Modern Design*, Thames & Hudson, London, 1991

Dunne, A., *Hertzian Tales: Electronic Products, Aesthetic Experience, and Critical Design*, The MIT Press, Cambridge, Mass., 2008

Dunne, A. and Raby, F., *Design Noir: The Secret Life of Electronic Objects*, Birkhauser, Munich, 2001

Fairs, M., *Twenty-first Century Design*, Carlton Books, London, 2006

Fiell, C. and Fiell, P., *Design Handbook (Icons)*, Taschen, Koln, 2006

Fiell, C. and Fiell, P., *Design Now: Designs for Life – From Eco-design to Design-art*, Taschen, Koln, 2007

Fiell, C. and Fiell, P., *Design of the 20th Century*, Benedikt Taschen Verlag, Koln, 1999

Fuad-Luke, A., *The Eco-Design Handbook: A Complete Sourcebook for the Home and Office*, Thames & Hudson, London (3rd edition), 2009

Fukasawa, N., *Naoto Fukasawa*, Phaidon Press, London, 2007

Fukasawa, N. and Morrison, J., *Super Normal: Sensations of the Ordinary*, Lars Muller Publishers, Baden, Switzerland (2nd extended edition), 2007

Fulton Suri, J., *Thoughtless Acts?*, Chronicle Books, San Francisco, 2005

Goodwin, K., *Designing for the Digital Age: How to Create Human-Centered Products and Services*, Wiley, New Jersey, 2009

Hallgrimsson, Bjarki, *Prototyping and Modelmaking for Product Design*, Laurence King Publishing, London, 2012

Henry, Kevin, *Drawing for Product Designers*, Laurence King Publishing, London, 2011

Heskett, J., *Toothpicks and Logos*, Oxford University Press, Oxford, 2002

Hudson, J., *Process 2nd edition: 50 Product Designs from Concept to Manufacture*, Laurence King Publishing, London, 2011

Hudson, J., *1000 New Designs 2 and Where to Find Them: A 21st Century Sourcebook*, Laurence King Publishing, London, 2010

IDEO, *IDEO Methods Cards*, William Stout Architectural Books, San Francisco, 2002

Jones, J.C., *Design Methods: Seeds of Human Futures*, John Wiley & Sons, Chichester, 1970

Jordan, P., *An Introduction to Usability*, Taylor and Francis, London, 1998

Jordan, P., *Designing Pleasurable Products*, Taylor and Francis, London, 2002

Julier, G., *The Culture of Design*, Sage Publications, London, 2000

Kahn, K.B. (ed.), *The PDMA Handbook of New Product Development*, John Wiley & Sons, New York, 2004

Koskinen, I., Zimmerman, J., Binder, T., Redstrom, J. and Wensveen, S., *Design Research Through Practice: From the Lab, Field, and Showroom*, Morgan Kaufmann, Burlington, 2011

Lawson, B., *How Designers Think, The Design Process Demystified*, Butterworth Architecture, Oxford, 1990

Lefteri, C., *Making It: Manufacturing Techniques for Product Design, 2nd edition*, Laurence King Publishing, London, 2012

Lefteri, C., *Materials for Inspirational Design*, Rotovision Publishers, Hove, 2006

Lorenz, C., *The Design Dimension: Product Strategy and the Challenge of Global Marketing*, Blackwell Publishers, Oxford, 1986

Manzini, E., *The Material of Invention*, Arcadia, Milan, 1986

Moggridge, B., *Designing Interactions*, The MIT Press, Cambridge, Mass., 2006

Morris, R., *The Fundamentals of Product Design*, AVA Publishing, Lausanne, 2009

Morrison, J., *Everything But the Walls*, Lars Muller Publishers, Baden, Switzerland (2nd extended edition), 2006

Myerson, J., *IDEO: Masters of Innovation*, Laurence King Publishing, London, 2004

Noble, I. and Bestley, R., *Visual Research: An Introduction to Research Methodologies in Graphic Design*, AVA Publishing SA, 2005

Parsons, T., *Thinking: Objects – Contemporary Approaches to Product Design*, AVA Publishing, Lausanne, 2009

Pink, S., *Doing Visual Ethnography: Images, Media and Representation in Research*, Sage Publications., London, 2001

Potter, N., *What Is a Designer: Things, Places, Messages*, Hyphen Press, London (4th revised edition), 2008

Proctor, R., *1000 New Eco Designs and Where to Find Them*, Laurence King Publishing, London, 2009

Pye, D., *The Nature and Aesthetics of Design*, A. and C. Black Publishers, London, 2000

Redhead, D., *Products of Our Time*, Birkhauser Verlag AG, Munich, 1999

Rodgers, P., *Inspiring Designers*, Black Dog Publishers, London, 2004

Rodgers, P., *Little Book of Big Ideas: Design*, A. and C. Black Publishers, London, 2009

Rowe, P.G., *Design Thinking*, The MIT Press, Cambridge, Mass., 1987

Rodgers, P. and Milton, A. *Product Design*, Laurence King Publishing, London, 2011

Schön, D.A., *The Reflective Practitioner: How Professionals Think in Action*, Basic Books, New York, 1983

Schouwenberg, L. and Jongerius, H., *Hella Jongerius*, Phaidon Press., London, 2003

Slack, L., *What is Product Design?*, Rotovision Publishers, Hove, 2006

Sudjic, D., *The Language of Things*, Allen Lane Publishers, London, 2008

Thackara, J., *Design after Modernism: Beyond the Object*, Thames & Hudson, London, 1988

Thompson, R., *Manufacturing Processes for Design Professionals*, Thames & Hudson, London, 2007

Troika, *Digital by Design: Crafting Technology for Products and Environments*, Thames & Hudson, London, 2008

Ulrich, K.T. and Eppinger, S.D., *Product Design Development*, McGraw Hill, Cambridge, Mass., 2000

Whitely, N., *Design for Society*, Reaktion Books, London, 1993

Magazines

Abitare
www.abitare.it

Arcade
www.arcadejournal.com

AXIS
www.axisinc.co.jp/english

Blueprint
www.blueprintmagazine.co.uk

Creative Review
www.creativereview.co.uk

Design Engineer
www.engineerlive.com/Design-
Engineer

Design Week
www.designweek.co.uk

Domus
www.domusweb.it

Dwell
www.dwell.com

Elle Decor
www.pointclickhome.com/elle_decor

Eureka
www.eurekamagazine.co.uk

Frame
www.framemag.com
FX
www.fxmagazine.co.uk

Icon
www.iconeye.com
Interni
www.internimagazine.it

Metropolis
www.metropolismag.com/cda

Neo2
www.neo2.es

New Design
www.newdesignmagazine.co.uk

Objekt
www.objekt.nl

Ottagano
www.ottagono.com

Surface
www.surfacemag.com

Wallpaper*
www.wallpaper.com

Websites

3D Modelling, Rapid Prototyping
Manufacturing Technology
www.3dsystems.com

100% Design
www.100percentdesign.co.uk

Architonic
www.architonic.com

Better Product Design
www.betterproductdesign.net

British Inventors Society
www.thebis.org/index.php

Centre for Sustainable Design
www.cfsd.org.uk

Cooper-Hewitt National Design
Museum, USA
www.cooperhewitt.org

Design & Art Direction (D&AD)
www.dandad.org

Design Boom
www.designboom.com

Design Classics Resource
www.tribu-design.com

Design Council
www.designcouncil.org.uk

Design Discussion Forum
www.nextd.org

Design Engine
www.design-engine.com

Design Magazine and Resource
www.core77.com

Design Management Institute
www.dmi.org

Design Museum, London
www.designmuseum.org

Design News for Design Engineers
www.designnews.com

Design Philosophy Papers
www.desphilosophy.com

Design Resource
www.designaddict.com

Design*Sponge
www.designsponge.blogspot.com

Designers Block
www.verydesignersblock.com/2009

Designers' Guide to Materials and Processes
www.designinsite.dk/htmsider/home.htm

Dexigner
www.dexigner.com

Ecology-derived Techniques for Design
www.biothinking.com/slidenj.htm

Educational Resource for Designers
www.thedesigntrust.co.uk

How Stuff Works
www.howstuffworks.com

Inclusive Design Toolkit
www.inclusivedesigntoolkit.com

Information/Inspiration Eco Design Resource
www.informationinspiration.org.uk

Institute of Nano Technology
www.nano.org.uk

International Contemporary Furniture Fair
www.icff.com/page/home.asp#

London Design Festival
www.londondesignfestival.com

Milan Furniture Fair (Salone Internazionale del Mobile)
www.cosmit.it

MoCo Loco
www.mocoloco.com

Modern World Design Eco-Design Links
www.greenmap.com/modern/resources.html

New Designers
www.newdesigners.com

Participatory Design Methods
interliving.kth.se/publications/thread/index.html

Places and Spaces
www.placesandspaces.com

Red Dot Design Museum
en.red-dot.org/design.html

Royal Society of Arts
www.rsa-design.net

Showroom of UK Designers' Work
www.designnation.co.uk

The Story of Stuff
www.storyofstuff.com

Stylepark
www.stylepark.com

Victoria and Albert Museum
www.vam.ac.uk

Vitra Design Museum
www.design-museum.de

Webliography of Design
www.designfeast.com

Design competitions

Braun Prize
www.braunprize.com

Design & Art Direction (D&AD), Student Awards
www.dandad.org

Good Design Award
www.g-mark.org

IF Concept Award
www.ifdesign.de

Materialica Design Award
www.materialicadesign.com

Muji Award
www.muji.net/award

Promosedia International
www.promosedia.it

Red Dot Design Award
www.red-dot.de

Royal Society of Arts
Design Directions Student Awards
www.rsa-design.net

Useful addresses

Australia

Powerhouse Museum
500 Harris Street, Ultimo
PO Box K346, Haymarket
Sydney, NSW 1238
www.powerhousemuseum.com

Belgium

Design Museum
Jan Breydelstraat 5
9000 Ghent
design.museum.gent.be

Canada

DX: The Design Exchange
234 Bay Street, PO Box 18
Toronto Dominion Centre
Toronto, ON M5K 1B2
www.dx.org

Denmark

The Danish Museum of Art & Design
Bredgade 68/1260, København K
www.kunstindustrimuseet.dk

Germany

Bauhaus-Archiv Museum of Design
Klingelhöferstrasse 14
D-10785 Berlin
www.bauhaus.de/english/index.htm

Die Neue Sammlung
Barer Strasse 40
80333 Munich
www.die-neue-sammlung.de

Red Dot Design Museum
Gelsenkirchener Strasse 181
45309 Essen
en.red-dot.org/371.html

Vitra Design Museum
Charles-Eames-Str. 1
D-79576 Weil am Rhein
www.design-museum.de

Ireland

Institute of Designers Ireland
FX2 The Fumbally Exchange
Fumbally Square
Dublin 8
http://idi-design.ie/

Mexico

Mexican Museum of Design
Francisco I. Madero No. 74
Colonia Centro Histûrico
Delegaciûn CuauhtÈmoc
Mèxico D.F, C.P. 06000
www.mumedi.org

Singapore

Red Dot Design Museum
28 Maxwell Road
Singapore, 069120
www.red-dot.sg/concept/museum/
main_page.htm

United Kingdom

Chartered Society of Designers
1 Cedar Court, Royal Oak Yard
Bermondsey Street
London, SE1 3GA
www.csd.org.uk

Design Museum
28 Shad Thames
London, SE1 2YD
www.designmuseum.org

Geffrye Museum
Kingsland Road
London, E2 8EA
www.geffrye-museum.org.uk

Institution of Engineering Designers
Courtleigh, Westbury Leigh, Westbury
Wiltshire, BA13 3TA
www.ied.org.uk

Victoria and Albert Museum
Cromwell Road
London, SW7 2RL
www.vam.ac.uk

United States

Cooper-Hewitt, National Design Museum
2 East 91st Street, New York
NY 10128
www.cooperhewitt.org

The Eames Office
850 Pico Boulevard, Santa Monica
CA 90405
www.eamesoffice.com

Industrial Designers Society of America
45195 Business Court, Suite 250, Dulles
VA 20166-6717
www.idsa.org

Museum of Arts and Design
2 Columbus Circle, New York
NY 10019
www.madmuseum.org

Museum of California Design
P.O. Box 361370, Los Angeles
CA 90036
www.mocad.org

Museum of Design, Atlanta
285 Peachtree Center Avenue
Marquis Two Tower, Atlanta
Georgia 30303-1229
www.museumofdesign.org

New Museum
235 Bowery, New York
NY 10002
www.newmuseum.org

Smithsonian Institution
PO Box 37012
SI Building, Room 153, MRC 010
Washington D.C. 20013-7012
www.si.edu

UC Davis Design Museum and Design Collection
145 Walker Hall, University of California
One Shields Avenue, Davis
CA 95616
www.designmuseum.ucdavis.edu/
index.html

Index

Picture credits

The author and publisher would like to thank the following institutions and individuals who provided images for use in this book. In all cases, every effort has been made to credit the copyright holders, but should there be any omissions or errors the publisher would be pleased to insert the appropriate acknowledgment in subsequent editions of this book.

Front cover
Æ+Y phone by Yves Béhar, fuseproject, for Æsir Copenhagen. Photographer Jonathan de Villiers
Back cover
Sketches courtesy of Tom Dixon

8 Courtesy of University of Northumbria School of Design
10 Design process cards by Jonny Weir
11 Methods cards courtesy of IDEO
13 © Which? magazine
15 Diagrams courtesy of Alex Milton and Suzanne Martin
20 © Melis82/Dreamstime Stock Photos & Stock Free Images
21 Courtesy of James Shutt
22 Courtesy of IDEO
23 Courtesy of Ana Alves and Rui Alves, University of Madrid
24 & 25 Courtesy of University of Northumbria School of Design
27 & 28 Courtesy of James Shutt
29 © James Leynse/Corbis
30 © OMA
31 © Mudpie
32 Courtesy of Isaac Teece
33 Courtesy of Æsir; photographer Jonathan de Villiers
34 Courtesy of La Triennale Design Museum, Martí Guixé sketch
35 (top) sketches courtesy of Tom Dixon; (middle) sketches courtesy of Tokujin Yoshioka; (bottom) sketches courtesy of Patricia Urquiola/Kartell
36 (top) Courtesy of Tom Dixon; (bottom) Courtesy of University of Northumbria School of Design
37 Courtesy of PearsonLloyd
38 & 39 courtesy of IDEO
40 & 41 courtesy of Sense Worldwide
43 © Josef Mohyla/iStockphoto
44 © Pedro Castellano/iStockphoto
46 © Sony Corporation

47 Courtesy of Lizette Reitsma
48 Courtesy of Deutsche Telekom Laboratories
49 (Clockwise, top to bottom) Samsung GT i9020 Nexus S and Samsung Infuse 4G SGH courtesy of Samsung; Nokia Lumia 800 courtesy of Nokia; Sony Xperia ArcS courtesy of Sony
50 © urbancow/iStockphoto
52 © Frank Delm/Getty Images
53 Courtesy of University of Northumbria School of Design
55 © George Peters/iStockphoto
57 (top) Wordle™; (bottom) Angela Gray
58 © TommL/iStockphoto
61 Courtesy of Bill Gavers
62 & 63 images © Adidas
68 © Yevgen Timashov/iStockphotos
70 Courtesy of University of Northumbria School of Design
71 © Erik Bohemia courtesy of University of Northumbria School of Design
72 (left) courtesy of Rory Hyde; (right) courtesy of Vola Nito Rapsel
73 © Joos Mind/Getty Images
74 (top to bottom) logo designs © Adidas; © Reebok; © IBM: IBM and the IBM logo are trademarks of International Business Machines Corp., registered in many jurisdictions worldwide; © Google
75 Courtesy of Isaac Teece
76 Courtesy of Tom Harper, Edinburgh College of Art
78 Courtesy of Rosie MacCurrach
79 (top) photograph by Mischa Haller www.mischaphoto.com; (middle and bottom) Andrea Dall'Olios's Home Interior Trend book, S/S 2010
82 Photograph by Mischa Haller www.mischaphoto.com
85 Courtesy of Héctor Serrano and Victor Vina
87 Courtesy of Seymourpowell
89 Courtesy Isabel Krumholz Adler MSc and Brenda de Figueiredo Lucena MSc, MJV Tecnologia e Inovação
92 Courtesy of Jonny Weir
94 One Laptop Per Child XO Computer, Yves Béhar/fuseproject
95 Part tables, Stephen Burks
96 Courtesy of Deutsche Telekom Laboratories
97 (top) Edward Barber and Jay Osgerby's De La Warr Pavilion Chair;

(bottom) Courtesy of University of Northumbria School of Design
99 Courtesy of Scholten & Baijings
100 Tom Beiling, Deutsche Telekom Laboratories
101 Courtesy of University of Northumbria School of Design
102 & 103 Courtesy of Seymourpowell
104 & 105 Tom Beiling, Design Research Lab
106 Courtesy of IDEO
107 Courtesy of Andreia Chaves, Freedom of Creation
108 Courtesy of Design Partners
109 © Lionel T. Dean
110 & 111 Courtesy of Dyson
112 & 113 Courtesy of OXO Good Grips
114 & 115 Courtesy of Pili Wu
116 & 117 Courtesy of Proboscis
118 Courtesy of Deutsche Telekom Laboratories
119 (top) Courtesy of Wataru Watanabe
120 © BMW AG
122 © BMW AG
123 Courtesy of Design Research Lab and Deutsche Telekom Laboratories
124 Courtesy of PearsonLloyd
125 Courtesy of Sir Chris Bonington
126 & 127 courtesy of PearsonLloyd
129 (top) © Maurice Volmeyer/ Shutterstock; (bottom) © Vladislav Gajic/Shutterstock
130 & 131 Mini E © BMW AG
132 & 133 Courtesy of Berghaus
134 & 135 Courtesy of PearsonLloyd
137 Courtesy of Will Mitchell
138 Courtesy of Front, Höganäs Keramik. Photograph by Anna Lönnerstam
141 Courtesy of Will Mitchell
143 Courtesy of Max Lamb
144 © Jasmin Awad/iStockphoto
145 © Adidas
148 & 149 Courtesy of Seren
150 & 151 Courtesy of Land Rover;
151 (top right) © Nick Dimbleby
156 © Brian A Jackson/Shutterstock
157 Courtesy of Propeller Design Team and Kapsel Multimedia AB
159 Courtesy of Seren
161 Courtesy of Robert Sloan
163 Entropia Light by Lionel T. Dean
166 & 167 © OMA
168 & 169 Courtesy of Cosmit
170 & 171 Courtesy of Jonny Weir
172 & 173 Courtesy of James Shutt

Acknowledgments

Paul Rodgers and Alex Milton would like to express their gratitude to all of the staff, students and their colleagues at Northumbria University, Heriot-Watt University, Edinburgh College of Art and the National College of Art and Design, Ireland.

The authors would also like to thank all of those designers who contributed their wonderful images of work and in particular to those who also gave their time to discuss and provide constructive thoughts and feedback as the book developed.

Alex Milton would especially like to thank Charlie Francis, Nik Finney, Suzanne Martin, Paul Kerlaff and Fiona Duff. Paul Rodgers would especially like to thank Alison, Charlie and Max for their continual support and Andy Tennant, Craig Bremner, Joyce Yee, Giovanni Innella and Freddie Yauner for their advice and help while putting this book together.

Finally, Alex and Paul would like to thank Gaynor Sermon and the team at Laurence King for helping them to complete their second book.